Copyright © 2019 by Party Girls On Purpose Pty Ltd

All rights reserved. No part of this publication may be reproduced, stored in a retrieval system, or transmitted in any form or by any means, electronic, mechanical, photocopying, recording or otherwise, without the prior written permission from the publisher.

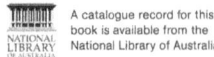
A catalogue record for this book is available from the National Library of Australia

Cover Illustration Copyright © Cat Louise Design
Graphic designer Aaron Vong design
Cover design and production by Self-publishing Lab
Book illustrations by Cat Louise Design
Editing by Caryn Stevens and Kat Millar.

ISBN:
978-1-925471-37-3 (pbk)
978-1-925471-37-3 (ebk)

Disclaimer: All the information, techniques, skills and concepts contained within this publication are of the nature of general comment only and are not in any way recommended as individual advice. The intent is to offer a variety of information to provide a wider range of choices now and in the future, recognising that we all have widely diverse circumstances and viewpoints.

Should any reader choose to make use of the information contained herein, this is their decision, and the contributors (and their companies), authors and publishers do not assume any responsibilities whatsoever under any condition or circumstances. It is recommended that the readers obtain their own independent advice.

First Edition 2019

Testimonials

Party Girls On Purpose is a breath of fresh air in the personal development space. It's not only filled with practical, doable steps, but fun and inspiring stories. Lauren's cheeky and playful humor is delightful and entertaining. The action points and examples bring it to life. Great, insightful read for all women wanting a better life"
 —Kat Millar, *Amplify Your Influence*, Sydney Australia

I love how the book relates goal setting and motivation to my every day life.
 It makes it relatable and attainable rather than isolating people with fancy mumbo jumbo. I love to party and know I'm good at It and I have learnt I can use the skills I have for having a good night out to help me create a great life too. Every day events and situations that are easy to recognize and you can see yourself in and reflect on in your own life, and I love

an excuse to bring out the party girl and celebrate my successes.
—Lizzie Worsdell, Actor/Producer, London UK

Lauren has written a must read for the dedicated Party girl who wants success in her life not just her night!

When it comes to attracting what you want there are so many writers that claim their way can make it happen, Lauren's fun filled guide to creating the life of your dreams in 5 simple steps is delightfully fun, opening the mind to believe that every GREAT night out develops your skills for a GREAT life. That you have potential to manifest whatever you have ever wanted!
—Louisa Shell, *The Modist,* Dubai

Dedication

I dedicate this book to all the party girls out there who are looking for more in life and want to live for more than just the weekend.

The dreamers who are willing to take action to make those dreams a reality, who know there's more to life and will seek people, books and learning's to help them achieve them.

For these party girls on purpose I raise my glass of champagne and cheers to these, successful fun and fabulous ladies.

I also dedicate this to my wonderful family my mum and dad who put up with the party girl before she was on purpose for many many years!! Late night pick ups from town or disappearing for days on end and a moody tired daughter from Monday to Thursday, thank you for still loving me and believing in me supporting me and just being bloody great parents I love you so much.

And to my sister Sarah from the UK to Australia, we have shared a lot of great moments, you have supported and lifted me up, I love you so much and thank you for my beautiful nephew Oscar.

My little bro James thanks for being you and enjoy the travel and adventures you're now on,

To Steph Toogood for being my first mentor and giving me a love for travel.

Paul Gillies who gave me my first business to learn and grow from.

And Jody Coker who made me learn how to run a business I will be forever grateful.

To Louisa Shell who had the book the magic in her room that I borrowed and caused the biggest shift in my life to date. If we hadn't been writing our gratitude's and sharing our daily magic encounters I may never be where I am today so thank you Lou Lou.

And to all my great friends in the UK and Australia who I have partied with over the years some amazing memories and blurry nights but this book was created off the back of those fun nights, drinking, dancing and talking about our hopes and dreams until the early hours and other times just talking s@*t!! Here's to always having fun and always being the life and souls of the party while doing what we love!!

GO TO

PARTYGIRLSONPURPOSE.COM

for FREE access to AMAZING WORKSHEETS
use them and the GREAT formula to
get transformational results..

Party Girls On Purpose also
offer ongoing education

LIVE TRAINING with Author
Lauren Victoria Ellingham
Go in depth like never before into the PGOP
GREAT formula with live lessons, work
books and guided visualization sessions.

1 session a week over 5 weeks with a
live Q & A at the end to ask anything
you want about the FORMULA and how
to become a party girl on purpose.

1 day Masterminds and Retreats with a balance
of work and celebrating our successes in style.

Go to
PartyGirlsOnPurpose.com
for more information or to register interest.

Table of Contents

Foreword   xiii
Introduction   1
About this book   4
Living for the weekend   6
A Brief Background   9
Responsible Alcohol Consumption and the Class-A Team Warning   19
Who is a Party Girl on Purpose?   22
The G.R.E.A.T Formula   24

PILLAR ONE: GRATITUDE   29
    Make a Grateful List   30
    Your Internal Roller Coaster   35
    Appreciate the Lesson   37
    Appreciate What You Have   38
    Good Vibrations   40
       Family   46
       Work   47
       Social life   48

Relationships	49
Health	50
Finances	51
Summary	53
PILLAR TWO: RELAXATION / CHILL OUT	56
Me Time	57
Go Off the Grid	58
Say NO to Distractions	60
TAME THE BEAST	63
Relax and Recharge	64
Chill	66
Mini chills	69
Medium chills	70
Maximum chills	71
Mega chills	72
Day after the Night before	73
Summary	74
PILLAR THREE: EVALUATION / SET GOALS / INTENTIONS	77
Goals and Intentions	78
Party Girl Masterminds	79
Write Down Your Goals	80
Material World	88

Goals in All Areas	89
Material goals	92
Career goals	93
Relationship goals	94
Financial goals	95
Spiritual/self-improvement goals	96
Health and wellbeing goals	97
Summary	98
PILLAR FOUR: ACTION	100
Life Rewards Action	101
Action Equals Energy	102
Learning for Life	104
Transfer Your Skills	105
Action Worksheet	112
Monday	112
Tuesday	112
Wednesday	113
Thursday	113
Friday	113
Summary	114
PILLAR FIVE: TARGET / FOCUS / NOT GIVING UP	117
Pay Attention to Your Self-Talk	118
Focus on What You Want	119

Ignore Distractions	121
Use Setbacks as Feedback	122
Become an Expert	124
Star power	125
Worksheet	130
Summary	132

Party Queen and Boss Babe	
Final Thoughts	133
About the Author	137
References to the Sources of the Quotes Mentioned in the Book.	141
Glossary	151

Foreword

I wrote this book originally for past me, who sat and cried in a bed room after reading a book called the Magic by Rhonda Byrne, after that day something switched in me that could never go back and I didn't want it to.

It started me on a journey of personal development and study, I discovered many new teachers and learned lots of valuable lessons.

I struggled sometimes with some content in the first year, as it was as all so new.

I would describe it as airy-fairy or hippy dippy out there (I love this stuff now), then there was the other side that was so scientific or required lots of time and written work. Me being me wanted the quick route to success or the elevator to the penl house straight away.

That didn't happen and in a way I'm glad because I may have missed out on some of the great lessons and experience that I have been very blessed to have.

What I did learn over the years of discovery is that everyone is telling you the same thing, the wheel isn't broken there's no need to fix it and it works, it does, amazingly every time. You just need to make small adjustments in the way you think, what you believe. If you get clear on what you want and you can achieve, you will experience amazing results.

Party girls on purpose was started after a seminar when I was told to work out what I was good at and what I had the best experience in, I thought about it and what kept coming up was partying and socializing.

I can't make a career out of that I'm no Kim Kardashian or Paris Hilton I thought, but the more I thought about it, relaxed on the idea, the more it came together and I realized that it was the same behaviors and practices that I used to have a great night out that were basic lessons, starting points in personal development.

I had been looking for something simple to continue my learning after discovering about universal laws, manifesting and mindset, so I decided to write a book for my fellow party girls that have just started their journey of personal development and need lessons and actions to help them on their way that will take them to bigger and better things.

FOREWORD

The GREAT formula are your 5 personal development steps to get you to the successful life you have always dreamed about, simple easy steps that get you going in the right direction and if life gets to busy or in the way you can come back to, to follow to get you back on track.

Even if you have been a student in personal development for a while sometimes its good to re evaluate and to realign your self with your dreams and goals and keep you on track for success so this book is for you too.

I hope you enjoy this book, have fun reading it and take the time, your time, to complete the work sheets to give you some confidence, strategies, clarity and a plan to reach for the stars, dream big and be the most successful you, along with being a fabulous party girl on purpose.

PARTY GIRLS ON PURPOSE

Be a Party Queen and a Boss

Introduction

This book is for the women who are the life and soul of the party ,

It is for women who want to live an abundant life, full of success in all areas and have a great time doing it.

In this book, I show you how to use your already-amazing party girl skills to achieve your dreams, using the GREAT formula to show you a GREAT night can lead to a GREAT life.

To get started, I invite you to take the party girls on purpose test.

How many below relate to you?

★ You love to have fun
★ You play often and get others in a playful mood
★ You're a social queen who makes everyone feel special
★ You dream of success and having everything your heart desires

PARTY GIRLS ON PURPOSE

- ★ You're the first to hit the dance floor
- ★ You're socially an A-plus achiever
- ★ You love laughing and you're fun to be around
- ★ You're full of love for all life has to offer and like to share your happiness with others
- ★ You're open-minded, and always looking to improve yourself
- ★ You're energetic with a contagious lust for life

If you said yes to more than 5, this book is for you!

And this book will show you how to be a party girl on purpose.

Party girls on purpose are grateful for what they have in their life, they chill out often, have clear short and long-term goals, are up for any challenge and continually take action to achieve their biggest dreams and desires. They have their eye on the prize and stay focused no matter what life throws at them.

Small setbacks don't get them down; they just bounce back and try another way. They're always willing to learn and improve themselves.

I can help you get on track to living a life on purpose: with fun, freedom, friends, and lots of reasons for popping champagne. You just need to learn how to start on a new adventurous path, get on purpose

INTRODUCTION

and live life on your terms. Being on purpose means that every day can feel like a weekend, with plenty of opportunities to celebrate your successes.

About this book

Use Your Party Girl Skills to Achieve a Great Life

I want you to feel empowered to be able to achieve anything.

You're allowed to have everything you want in life, which is possible if you:

- ★ Utilise your skills and achievements.
- ★ Focus on gratitude
- ★ Don't sweat the small stuff (save that for the dance floor)
- ★ Chill out and trust your inner voice
- ★ Set and write down your short and long-term goals in all areas of your life
- ★ Set an intention to succeed in attaining your goals and feel confident and certain that you will

ABOUT THIS BOOK

- ★ Take action every day, even if it's just small steps, so your uphill struggle turns into an elevator ride to the penthouse
- ★ Maintain focus on what you want to achieve.

You can have anything and everything you set your heart or mind on.

I'm going to give you the steps to go for it, and not be afraid to celebrate the successes along the way.

Maybe the thought has crossed your mind that you should stop being a social queen; that it has been achieving success has been hindered by your love of socialising. I can tell you this isn't the case. You can achieve anything you desire by utilising the habits you've honed through creating great nights out now ensuring a good time for everyone.

In other words, you can become a party girl on purpose.

I will admit to not being on purpose for a long time. I got on purpose when I discovered personal development.

Personal Development is the conscious pursuit of personal growth by expanding self-awareness and knowledge and improving personal skills.

I found that if I transferred the party skills and strategies that I used to create the best nights out to other areas of my life, I could also achieve success for a great life. This is what I will share with you in the book, so that you can too.

Being a party girl isn't as easy as some might think. It's not all nightclubs, bars, beaches, festivals and VIP areas. It requires skills. Party girls need determination, focus, and most of all, endurance. Socialising, networking, being fabulous and dancing until dawn, with the possibility of doing it all over again the next day, is no mean feat.

It's about having a good time with friends and it has been making a night/weekend last as long as possible, to squeeze the most out of it and have the best time and so it should be for all of your life now not just the weekend.

Living for the weekend

If you were like me and not on purpose, your mantras probably sound a lot like this:

- ★ I live for the weekend. Long live the weekend!
- ★ I hate Mondays
- ★ On Wednesday I celebrate hump days.
- ★ Thank God it's Friday!

ABOUT THIS BOOK

So are you socialising and partying for fun and celebration or to escape from the mundane life you have created for yourself?

Are you in a job you hate that pays the bills?

Do you have a healthy bank balance or always in the red?

Do you wake up every morning excited for what the day may bring, or dread another day of the same?

Do you blow nearly an entire week's salary on partying and can only go on holidays when you have enough for a bigger escape?

If you're living the life from Friday to Sunday, but come Monday morning you feel unfulfilled and depressed, you probably need the tips I'm going to share with you in this book.

If around you, you see everyone else doing the same thing, you may begin to wonder if you're selfish to want every day to be amazing and is that even possible?

You love a good party, but there comes a point where you feel there's something missing, and you might ask yourself why you spend your weekends escaping your weeks. You begin to wonder what it would be like to live a life you love every day, with the freedom to do what you want, when you want, because when you're doing what you love, there's no motivation needed.

To achieve this goal and create balance, you must take your partying skills to other areas so all aspects of your life are as good as your weekends.

This book is an easy guide to not only have a fabulous weekend...but to live a fabulous life.

A Brief Background

A Brief History of a Party Girl Off Purpose Who Found Magic, and Purpose Followed

It was a cold June afternoon in Sydney Australia in 2012 I was in my small, dim bedroom in Bondi. I was lying under the covers with tears in my eyes reading a book called *The Magic* by Rhonda Byrne (author of *The Secret*), which became the key to changing my life forever.

But first, let me rewind twenty-odd years previous to a girl who was always up for a party. Weekends would start Friday when I'd go out drinking be the last one standing, and turn into one long blur till Sunday.

I had my first drink at thirteen with some school friend in London. Then when I moved to the Isle of Wight at fourteen, I had found it hard being the new girl and fit in, but I made some older friends in the village of Porchfield, Kate and Deana, who were already drinking and smoking. So I did, too.

PARTY GIRLS ON PURPOSE

When I was only fifteen, I was going to night clubs with homemade fake ID, and by age sixteen I was attending illegal raves at an old fort run by bikers. My poor Mum and Dad never suspected. They thought I was staying at friends' houses. They knew I was resentful for being made to move from West London to the Island and was getting bullied at school, so I was given more freedom than most.

Socialising, dancing, drink, drugs, friends and after parties were how I lived my weekends. I was the queen of the party, enjoying drinking games and seeing what I could get away with and how high I could get.

During the week I worked at a leisure centre, which I liked and did other odd jobs, but I wasn't passionate about or inspired by them. My friends Lee and Nathan were DJ's, and we started organising events. I loved doing this, organising coaches to party on the mainland and running great events in our town, but though we tried to be successful, we never quite got there, and it fizzled out, we gave up.

I kept trying to find my purpose, but I'd start well then get bored. I was a lifeguard, receptionist, gym instructor, water aerobics instructor and duty manager…I tried them all, but nothing was more fun than partying on the weekend. That's when I looked

A BRIEF BACKGROUND

my best and had the best time dancing and laughing with friends into the small hours.

But I was drinking too much and doing as many party drugs as possible to escape my week, which left me with too many embarrassing stories to count. Like breaking into my friend Charlotte's house, even though I had her keys in my hand... and getting fired from a couple of jobs.

I thought I had found the career to take me to my successful life. I became a water aerobic trainer with Speedo and travelled to the USA a few times a year to attend conventions. I even won a presenter competition. The future was bright, but I made the mistake of partying before a training course in London, so I wound up missing my boat and never made it to the course. I lost my job, and at the time, I thought my future as well. I was devastated. With that job, my life was planned out as to what I'd be doing and where I'd be every year, and though it was more than I had on the island deep down, I knew I still wanted more.

I was now 30 and stressed out. My weekends didn't refresh me. I'd drink and party until Sunday night, so by Monday I was a wreck, Tuesday I'd be teary and emotional. Then I'd be moody and not fun to be around only starting to feel like me and productive again by Thursday and the week was almost over.

I had this vague fantasy of being rich and famous but no plan to get there. I've always been an ideas-person but was also full of self-doubt, so I'd have these great ideas and start a project, only to abandon it if it got too hard. Then I'd look back and think, *What if.*

I wasn't at all where I wanted to be in life. I desired success, money, and to travel and have adventures, but the only thing I was good at was partying.

I dreamed of going to Australia but thought I'd missed my chance. One day my friends, Becci and Ricky, who were already out there told me it was still possible. Could I do it? Move half way across the world and see what happened?

I had been working for a local radio station and one of the DJ Paul Gillies started a silent disco company became his event manager and lo I became his event manager and worked at major UK festivals which I loved but I wanted more. So without a thought to money or a job, I got my visa and made to plan.

I flew to Australia in November 2010 with my mate, Gemma, and figured I'd get a good job and start achieving that success I'd always wanted, with lots of money and adventure. I assumed since I was moving halfway across the world, this had to be it.

A BRIEF BACKGROUND

Well, it didn't go quite to plan, but my God, Sydney is a wonderful place to party. I arrived in summer with seven-hundred pounds to my name, which is around $1200 AUS. I wound up dancing on boat parties as we sailed past the Opera house, going to day festivals, spending New Year's Eve on a rooftop party in Sydney harbour, and going out to a club at 5am to party till midday on Sunday. Yet again, socially my life was going well, and I was having an amazing time, but I wasn't achieving success in any other areas of my life.

I loved being the party girl, and I think people could tell. You don't get the nickname "Latenight Lozza" from being the first one home with a cup of tea and a Panadol now do you?

Fast-forward back to 2012. I'd recently lost my sponsorship visa that was keeping me in Australia and had to become a student to stay. I had little money and was living in a house I couldn't afford in the smallest room that I resented, running a silent disco business I'd started with some friends in Aus and the help of Paul in the UK, but I was doing all the work by myself and feeling annoyed, as it was a lot of effort for minimal return. I was also for some strange reason very annoyed and resentful towards my sister for following me to Australia and jumping in on my dream and experience. In general, I was wondering what the hell I was doing with my life again,

Then I discovered the book *'The Magic'*. It was a revelation. I realised I had so much to be grateful for and started doing a few of the 28 practices mentioned in the book. My housemate, Louisa, and I agreed to do our gratitudes each morning and evening. We'd sit in the garden and talk about all of the amazing things that had happened to us that day, from being given free coffee, lunch being brought for us, to discounts on all of the items we wanted to buy in the shops. It doesn't seem like much, but it was truly magical, and it made me realise I had a lot to be grateful for and how much in my life I'd been appreciating.

I became interested in the Law of Attraction, which is the universal Law of Manifestation, and I learned about the magic of gratitude. Every page was a realisation, and I didn't want to put it down. When I finished it, I wanted to learn more, so my quest for personal development began…

About a month later, my friend Sean invited me to hear a speaker at a hotel in the CBD. This is when I was introduced to a man named Benjamin J Harvey from Authentic Education. He opened his talk about how we

A BRIEF BACKGROUND

should live our love every day, have the best life has to offer and not struggle and be unhappy,

I welled up immediately and knew I was in the right place. It's amazing how synchronicities happen once your mind expands. I went to many more of Ben's talks and signed up for my first course in 2012. I've now been a student of Authentic Education for six years plus. I can't praise them enough. It's through one of their courses in book writing that I discovered Author Express with the lovely Fiona Allen and got the inspiration to write this book.

From lessons learnt through Authentic Education and other Mentors, I developed a new attitude that translated into receiving higher salaries. I became a problem solver and was accountable for myself and those I was in charge of.

It also helped me make 'Silent Disco King Australia' number one for headphones hires in Australia. I wound up touring with Australia's largest music festival, Big Day Out, in 2013 and 2014, taking my sister with me. I realised how silly I had been feeling resentful for her following me. She continues to be a massive support, especially when living so far from the rest of our family. I love her being there for me and for giving me a little nephew. My little business took off and is still growing today. I went from a broke party girl to a sought-after Manager and successful Business Owner in a few short years.

I also have many personal development Mentors such as Dr John Demartini, also from the Secret who I love his talks about our highest values and Abraham Hicks, a creation of Esther and Jerry Hicks. I love the concept of focusing on what you really do want and not what you don't. It seems so easy but so amazing how if you pay attention to your thoughts they are focused more often than not on the negative. More recently, I've added Carl James Harvey (no relation to Ben), who runs an abundant book club that I'm a member of. He's all about being playful, abundant and successful. He mixes together fun and good vibes, with the application of what we learn in the books we read, as well as his love for hip hop music. He's a boss!

Oprah Winfrey also inspires me. She's a great believer in the power of gratitude, finding your purpose, and being the best you and finally Mel Robbins who's lessons on productivity and the 5 second rule get you taking action on your goals.

It's through these mentors, and many others, after reading hundreds of books on the subject, watching hours of online content, attending seminars and

A BRIEF BACKGROUND

webinars and reading article after article, that I saw clearly how the laws of abundance and attraction are always working for you, whether you realise it or not.

All of these people are saying similar things. You just need to hear it from the one who resonates with you.

In June 2017, (June seems to be an inspirational month for me), I was at the Sheraton on the Park Hotel in Sydney CBD. I was swimming in the beautiful pool just after coming out the steam room, when the idea for the G.R.E.A.T. formula came to me, and I wrote them down immediately. The title, *Party Girls on Purpose*, had come to me months before in the early hours while lying in my bed in my beautiful house in Bellevue Hill working on a personal development project. So this book was coming together through a time of inspiration, and more realisations of how being a successful party girl had brought me to a place where I was on purpose and working towards the life I'd always dreamed of.

I've gathered together all of my years of learning and education to create a simple step-by-step process for women who have discovered personal development and want a simple guide to follow to get the best success results fast.

I hope it resonates with you and will create the big shift as you continue on your own journey of self-discovery and development. You don't have to work decades in an unfulfilling job to pay the bills, only to retire and struggle on a pension, having feelings of waste and regret.

This may sound harsh, but I'm trying to paint a clear picture, so you understand your life doesn't have to be this way.

Through my education, I've found five key elements you're already using as a successful party girl, that are essential to creating the life you love. You can be as successful in your work, health, relationships and career to as you are at partying and socialising. It took me a while, but I figured it out, and I'm going to share some of the most effective yet simple tools that I've learned, so you can accelerate your success!

I want to help you achieve your goals using the keen party skills you've already developed. By getting on purpose, you will light up brighter than a dance floor at a retro club on a Saturday night.

Once I show you how efficiently you're already using your skills to ensure the perfect night out, and how you can use them in other areas of your life, you'll become a *party girl on purpose.*

Responsible Alcohol Consumption and the Class-A Team Warning

Alcohol is usually a part of the going-out experience, but as you know: overdoing it can cause great nights to go bad in a blurry haze of *What did I do last night?* I'm not here to preach to you about your alcohol intake, but I will say that if you want to be an effective party girl on purpose, you need to keep your wil, and wits, about you!

Drugs and alcohol can be used as a crutch for confidence you don't feel you possess.

A delicious cocktail is created to be enjoyed, not downed to get you drunk quickly, so you're brave enough to talk to people. You don't need to do this. Confidence comes from the inside when you're on purpose and doing what you love.

Slurring, staggering and repeating yourself has no value. Party girls on purpose are the life and soul of a party, but this doesn't include having your hair held back in a toilet cubicle or being taken home early because you can no longer stand on your own two feet.

Any day/night out you can't remember isn't a success. It means you lost control yourself, and you don't want that to be your story. I don't say this to make you feel guilty – not at all! I have been there and I get it. This is about focusing forward on what you truly want and deserve. And I know that you're more than that.

You want to be a fabulous networking master; a seductress and fabulous dancer. Too much alcohol makes you think you're the best, but call up one of your sober friends the next day, the one you were trying to tell you life goals to (while slurring and spitting on them with red wine lips), and you'll hear the truth. Or talk to the guys you tried to seduce with lipstick smeared around your mouth and were grinding against to the latest dance track, because you thought you could do the singer's sexy dance way better than she did. (hint: you probably couldn't, but hey, we've all been there!). If you're lying on your friend's sofa drooling, you're not being a party girl on purpose.

Regarding recreational drugs: a party girl on purpose needs to be on form and in control at all times. When mixing drugs and alcohol, you'll discover there's a fine line between being the life of the party,

RESPONSIBLE ALCOHOL CONSUMPTION AND THE CLASS-A TEAM WARNING

where you're witty and entertaining, to being a crazy, jaw-swinging, eye-rolling mess.

Have fun. Be fabulous, be flirty, and be in control of you. That's the true nature of being a *party girl on purpose.*

Who is a Party Girl on Purpose?

The difference between a party girl and a party girl on purpose

PARTY GIRL	PARTY GIRL ON PURPOSE
Lives for the weekend and is only happy when she's partying.	Lives and loves her life, while celebrating her successes
Hates Mondays, because she hates her job.	Wakes up every day knowing she's living the life she's chosen for herself doing what she loves.
Won't leave the party as she doesn't want it to end and return to boring reality	Knows when the party is over and it's time to go home as she has bigger priorities to get on with.
Goes on holiday to escape her life.	Every day feels like a holiday.

WHO IS A PARTY GIRL ON PURPOSE?

Party girls on purpose are:

- ★ leaders
- ★ achievers
- ★ strong communicators
- ★ networkers
- ★ problem solvers
- ★ reliable
- ★ playful
- ★ fun
- ★ capable
- ★ always up for a challenge

If you don't feel your any of these yet, don't worry. This book will be the key to helping you get on track and become a *party girl on purpose*.

The G.R.E.A.T Formula

GREAT nights lead to a GREAT life

The G.R.E.A.T Formula

1. Gratitude

Gratitude is the foundation for changing your life. Appreciating what you have achieved in life so far, who you have in your life and what you have is the first steps. Acknowledging and feeling grateful for your life is powerful and once harnessed works magic.

2. Relaxation / Chill Out

More people are stressed and burnt out than ever before. When we are trapped in a cycle of stress and over work we are closed off to our inner guidance and creativity. Learn how to stop and chill out. Be open to your intuition and ideas, they are the key to achieving your dreams.

3. Evaluation / Goal setting

Look at what you have done and learnt so far. Note your achievements and work out where you want to go from here. What you would like to have, own, experience. Who you would like to do it all with. Get your goals down in all areas of your life so you are clear to yourself and the universe what you want.

4. Action

Simple, you get nowhere doing nothing. LIFE REWARDS ACTION so you're going to need to take some. Keep taking it until you get what you want. Then you keep taking more action as you move onto your next goal. Just keep moving forward.

5. Target and staying on track

Instant success is very rare. It's those that know what they want and don't let anyone get in their way who will be the winners in the end. There is no failure just feedback and using what you learn to continue on is key to great success. Keep at it until success is inevitable.

After reading, *The Magic*, I wanted to learn more about what to do with this newfound knowledge and how to get the best results fast.

I came across lots of amazing books by some great mentors, but nothing they revealed felt relevant to my background. Some were just too 'out there' for me and not coming from the same perspective I was, while others had detailed and complex steps that I didn't relate to, and felt would cause people to give up before they completed the entire process.

What I wanted was a set of simple steps that women who love to party and socialise could use to help them get on purpose and achieve the highest level of success.

I wanted to inspire these women to create a shift and realise it only requires a few tweaks to take their exceptional social skills and create an equally successful life in all areas.

By practicing my own principles, I came up with the G.R.E.A.T. formula.

It linked the skills that I used to have a great night out and converted them to create impressive achievements in all areas of life, in the fastest time possible. In other words, becoming a *party girl on purpose.*

The G.R.E.A.T. Process:

- ★ **Gratitude**
  By understanding and focusing on the power of gratitude, you can achieve anything you set your mind to and realise how much you have to be grateful for in your life already.
- ★ **Relaxation/chill out**
  Getting focused on yourself and into the right vibration to be aligned with the magic of the universe is where you tap in to your creativity and ideas.
- ★ **Evaluation / goal setting**
  Write down and continue to reference your goals, so the universe gets clear on what to send you.
- ★ **Action**
  Life rewards action. Big leaps will follow small steps. This principle is all about knowing the right quality action to take.
- ★ **Target / Focus**
  It's not enough to just target your goals. They require focus and determination to make them a reality and continue even when challenges come along.

So many people have dreams, but never get clear enough to follow through on them. By using these easy-to-follow steps, you'll be able to work out what you really want in life, start towards it and stay on target. All by using your current party girl skills to have the most fabulous life you can imagine.

Are you ready to become a party girl on purpose?

Let's get started!

PILLAR ONE
GRATITUDE

> *Gratitude turns what we have into enough, and more. It turns denial into acceptance, chaos into order, confusion into clarity...it makes sense of our past, brings peace for today, and creates a vision for tomorrow.*
> ~Melody Beattie

GRATITUDE *(noun)* The quality of being thankful; readiness to show appreciation for, and to return, kindness. *Synonyms*: appreciation, recognition, acknowledgement, hat tip, credit, regard, respect

A grateful party girl gains so much more to be thankful for than just a good night out when she expands her appreciation out to all other areas of her life.

At this point, you may feel you don't have much to be grateful for. You may not have the relationship, material things or circumstances you think you need to have to live your best life. But I'd encourage you to take a moment and truly look at where you are, what you do have, and the people you share your life with, and ask yourself, *"Do I truly have nothing to be grateful for?"*

I'm sure you'll agree that no matter how hard you feel life is right now, there is plenty to be grateful for.

Putting aside the thank god it's Friday feeling every week. I can remember going over my gratitude list almost subconsciously as I got ready to go out. Waves of gratitude would wash over me while thinking about the good times ahead. It felt amazing!

Make a Grateful List

Do you have people in your life who make your days better? People you count on to cheer you up when you're going through hard times and celebrate your achievements with you?

Are you happy with your home, your car or your job? Or do you take them for granted and constantly complain about them?

Make a list of everything you have to be thankful for. You may be surprised to discover how great your life really is.

PILLAR ONE: GRATITUDE

★ **Friendships and relationships**

As a party girl out and about, your path will cross with many different people. Some will become lifelong friends, while others will be mates for the night; some you'll learn great lessons from, and some you'll have forgotten by the following day.

Being a social queen helps you create the eclectic tapestry of people you meet on your journey through life.

Those you've decided to become your close friends make you feel good, and because of that, you want to keep them happy. You share similar interests, you support each other, and you laugh together. They're your support unit and extended family. They have your back through the bad times and the good. They provide you with a reality check if you're not handling some of your life situations, such as work, your relationship, or your finances, as well as you could.

Spending time with them is fun. Before I got on purpose, during nights out, I would take a moment and think to myself, *"Wow, I love my friends. How amazing are they?"* Now it happens every time I go out and every time I think about them. I look around at them having a laugh, sharing a story or asking for help with an issue, and all I can think about is how grateful I am to have them in my life.

Take a moment to think of your friends and the good times you share. Is there a chance you would benefit from feeling grateful for them in your life more often?

★ **Family**

Despite the jokes people make about family and no matter how imperfect they are, your family can give you plenty of reasons to be grateful for them.

My dad would be the one to drop us into town and would sometimes pick us up in the early hours of the morning. I even remember one time after some Christmas Eve celebrations, my sister throwing up out the window of his car. He was my hero.

My mum would always make me a cup of tea or a full English breakfast when I was struggling with a hangover.

My sister and I shared many fun times and adventures as she moved to Australia shortly after me, and I'm grateful to have a close bond with her.

PILLAR ONE: GRATITUDE

My little bro even gave us lifts once he passed his driving test and was always willing to pick me up at all times of the day and night.

Even if you don't feel you've been blessed with the greatest family, I'm sure you can think of times to be grateful for them.

Who in your family are you grateful for, and how do they contribute to your life?

★ **Work**

There have been times in my life I wasn't totally fulfilled or happy by my work. But I was always appreciative of having a job and earning my own money. I was paid enough to cover my bills and also have fun. The world was my oyster, and that first weekend after payday always the best.

Do you have a job that helps you pay the bills and party on the weekend and go on holidays? Are you grateful for it, or are you waking up every morning hating your life?

The choice is yours whether to embrace the good in your life or only look at the bad.

★ **The little things**

Remember to be grateful for the little things. For instance, the weather. The rain in the UK can play havoc with your hair and clothing, so I was always grateful for the nice weather when I didn't have to wear a big coat that would cover up my beautiful dress or worry about my hair getting wet or blown away in the wind. Id love to know what other things you could be grateful for on a night out.

Other things to be thankful for would be:

- ❖ A short queue to get in or a queue jump
- ❖ A great camping spot near the festival site
- ❖ Taxis waiting when you want to go home or Uber (Lyft) prices not surging out of control
- ❖ A friendly taxi driver who turns your favourite music up so you can all sing out loud leaving you smiling and laughing on your way out.
- ❖ Meeting someone with potential or bumping into an old friend you haven't seen in ages
- ❖ Your friend lending you the perfect top to go with your new jeans
- ❖ The shoes you have wanted for ages but were too expensive suddenly go in the sale just before your night out!

There's a lot to be grateful for!

Party girls on purpose know to count their blessing and are always aware of what they've achieved and are grateful for.

PILLAR ONE: GRATITUDE

You may not have your dream house, car, partner or job... YET, but that shouldn't stop you from appreciating what you've already created in your life.

If you're a party girl on purpose, you're always aiming for bigger and better things, and when you do reach a goal, your first action is to remember to be thankful for it before celebrating your successes in *party girl on purpose* style.

Your Internal Roller Coaster

Many people say life is a roller coaster of highs and lows. If you find that true for you, gratitude is a great balancer. When something good happens, before you run around screaming with excitement, spend a little time writing down why you're grateful. This will help balance you out and make you truly realise you're deserving of it.

Did you know that seventy percent of all lottery winners have been declared bankrupt after winning vast sums of money and ended up worse off than before the win? There has to be something to this! I've heard personal development mentors say it's due to deserving beliefs and your body's chemistry.

Let me ask you this: If you won a million dollars, would your internal roller coaster be in a dip or sky-rocketing to the moon?

As they say, what goes up must come down, and when you start coming down from that high, you'll feel undeserving.

What was discovered is that these winners subconsciously sabotaged themselves by investing their money with people and companies that didn't have their best interest at heart.

Both Benjamin J. Harvey and Dr John Demartini have said that if you ever have a lottery win, before popping the champagne, you need to get out a pen and paper and write down at least two-hundred reasons why you deserve that money, so your mind can balance out the amazing win with gratitude and deservedness, and you won't become another statistic.

When I first heard about this, I found it fascinating. All of these stories of bad investments and unhappiness, when you'd think winning the lottery would be the best thing that could ever happen to someone.

On the flipside, if you're going through hard times and experiencing a dip in your life, before becoming all "Woe is me" and resorting to self-deprecation or self-pity, it's important to change your perception and figure out how this could be a blessing in disguise. You'll find that in the bigger picture, your situation is helping you rather than hindering you. Look back at incidents you thought meant the end of the world, such as losing a job, having a fall-out with a friend, or experiencing hard financial times. When you were going through it, you probably felt helpless and powerless. But perhaps these incidents have helped shape who you are and made you stronger.

These events are all part of life's journey. There will be highs and lows; how you deal with them will determine whether or not you grow. Sure, you can get caught up with resentment, bitterness, and self-pity and remain low energy, or you can become stronger and wiser and soar to new heights. As Dr John Demartini says, "You need to see things as on the way, not *in* the way".

Being grateful for both the good and bad times will have an amazing impact on your life and stop you from feeling like you're on a rollercoaster.

Appreciate the Lesson

Time is a great healer and teacher. Once the energy from these situations fades away, take a look back and consider the lessons they taught you.

Maybe that lost job led to a better one, where you were paid more to do what you really loved. It might have kick-started you to further your education or work on a project you'd been putting off that led to you following you passion, rather than just turning up for a pay packet.

Maybe that fallout with your friend brought you closer together, or you discovered that you'd grown apart due to your paths going in different directions, and new friendships were made that were more supportive and helped you grow.

Financial woes can lead to a better appreciation of money and learning how to manage it and create a positive financial mindset, where you save rather than consume.

Appreciate What You Have

In the world we live in, where people are glorified and become rich by seemingly doing nothing, you can be forgiven for sometimes feeling you're not getting where you want to be in life quick enough. That you're not keeping up with the Kardashians or the Joneses and end up feeling disappointed.

PILLAR ONE: GRATITUDE

But these thoughts of lack work against you, because it's hard to get more things to be grateful for when you're not thankful for what you already have. No matter how much you think you're not succeeding in attaining your goals, there's always something to be grateful for, even if it's just being alive, a sunny day, good health, and yes, even adversity.

Learning to appreciate what you have is powerful and leads to receiving more to be thankful for.

As a party girl on purpose, you get to see so much, but don't let life pass you by. Take the time to notice the little things to be thankful for. When you're sharing a laugh and enjoying yourself, breathe in and be grateful. Gratitude is a state of being and a great equaliser. Many personal development superstars recognise and teach about the power of being grateful for what you have in all areas of your life, such as:

- ★ social friendships
- ★ relationships,
- ★ financial
- ★ material items
- ★ health and wellbeing
- ★ vitality
- ★ career

Good Vibrations

One of the books that changed my life, *The Magic* by Rhonda Byrne, has twenty-eight gratitude practices that work magic and can completely change your perspective on life. I've personally used many of these practices at times when I needed to be grateful for what I had, as I felt like I didn't have much. These exercises got me to focus on what I did have rather than what I didn't, and to be more grateful. I can attest that it did work like magic and brought more for me to be grateful for.

Know that once you start, it's a continual journey to discover on a daily basis how wonderful your life is.

Being in gratitude makes you feel good, and feeling good puts you in a great vibration to bring about more good things. You need to think of gratitude as high vibration.

Try this: if something gets stuck in your mind that doesn't make you feel good or grateful, (low vibration) you need to break that pattern by becoming really present.

What I mean is to stop the negative thought by add becoming aware of the thought then doing something about it. If you're walking down the street, notice the blue sky, a colorful flower, a smile from someone you walk past or your favorite song playing in a shop.

PILLAR ONE: GRATITUDE

Start thinking about a loved one or a recent moment you shared with a friend that makes you feel good and smile. Think about anything to pivot your mind away from the negative pattern that was dominating your thoughts.

Small things can make you feel just as good.

I used these gratitude practices and started to experience mini miracles and things to be grateful for.

Action Steps

☑ **Morning gratitude list**
Each morning when you wake, write down three to five things you're grateful for. It can be where you live, your friends, family, a loving partner, a great job or your health. Then once you've listed them, take a little time to think about each one and really feel the warm feelings of gratitude inside you before moving on to the next. This will help you raise your vibration. Everyone is a vibrating being of energy, and the things you want in life are in the high vibrations, so starting your day in a high vibration will help you reach your dreams.

☑ Gratitude Glitter

If you'd like to think of yourself as a glittery Disney fairy, then this action is perfect for you!

There's always someone to be thankful for, whether it's a friend, family member, an extra-friendly ride service driver, or the barista who makes your coffee. Whenever you feel appreciative of these people, in your imagination sprinkle a little Gratitude glitter on them to add an extra POW to your gratitude.

You can also use this method on those who are having a bad day. Maybe you don't receive a smile back, or someone is rude to you. Instead of choosing to be hurt or angry, consider that maybe they're having a rough day, so go ahead and imagine you're sprinkling some extra glitter on them, and give them a smile and a thank you.

Gratitude glitter can be used on anyone, so enjoy spreading it around to add more thanks to your thank you's, in the hope it brings magic to someone you're grateful for or to send good vibes to those who aren't having their best day.

PILLAR ONE: GRATITUDE

☑ **Gratitude Rock**

This one was from a lovely story by Lee Brower in *The Secret* and is repeated in *The Magic*. It's about a father who'd seen Lee's segment about how he carried around a rock during one of his darkest times and how it reminded him to be grateful. So when this man's son got seriously sick to the point they thought he would die, he asked Lee to send him some rocks. The man used them as a reminder to be grateful for his son's recovery.

Once the child miraculously recovered, the father went on to sell gratitude rocks to the rest of his village who had seen the magic of the child coming back to health, when they thought he wouldn't make it.

You can get yours from the beach, a garden park, or river.

Once you've selected your thank you rock, clear a space and put it on your bedside table, next to your lamp. Then before you go to bed, take your rock in the palm of your hand, close your fingers around it, and look back over the good things that happened that day. Pick the one you're most thankful for say it out loud or in your head before putting it down and going to sleep.

This is a perfect way to end your day!

So you can get started straight away, for the next few pages, spend time listing your gratitude in the following areas:

- ❖ Family
- ❖ Work
- ❖ Social life
- ❖ Relationships
- ❖ Health
- ❖ Finances

If you can't think of anything to write on a particular subject, that's fine. You can always go back and add more, until you have a massive list of things to be grateful for to look back on.

Some people have a gratitude journal they write in each day, these pages are a great start. And when you look back on them upon rereading the book and doing these G.R.E.A.T. steps, you will appreciate how much more you have to be grateful for.

PILLAR ONE: GRATITUDE

FAMILY

PILLAR ONE: GRATITUDE

WORK

SOCIAL LIFE

RELATIONSHIPS

HEALTH

PILLAR ONE: GRATITUDE

FINANCES

Now that you are more aware of how you've been using gratitude for great nights out, and you have a list of gratitude's to build upon, it's time to refocus your energy.

Being happy and thankful while you're partying is fine, but if you want to be a party girl on purpose, you have to be grateful starting from when you get up.

PILLAR ONE: GRATITUDE

Summary

What if...

Before getting out of bed, you say THANK YOU for

- being alive
- the weather
- your comfy bed and safe home
- your job that supports you
- your family
- your friends
- your health
  - ❖ You pay attention to every person, place and thing you have to be grateful for and acknowledge them
  - ❖ When someone does something nice, like pays for lunch or gives you a ride home, you're completely present and say THANK YOU and truly mean it, rather than being on autopilot

By not just saying the words "Thank you" but adding the heartfelt meaning behind them, you will feel the difference, and so will they.

It's going to be a revelation how much you have to be grateful for if you haven't been feeling too appreciative for what you already have.

> *Be thankful for what you have; you'll end up having more. If you concentrate on what you don't have, you will never, ever have enough.*
> **~Oprah Winfrey**

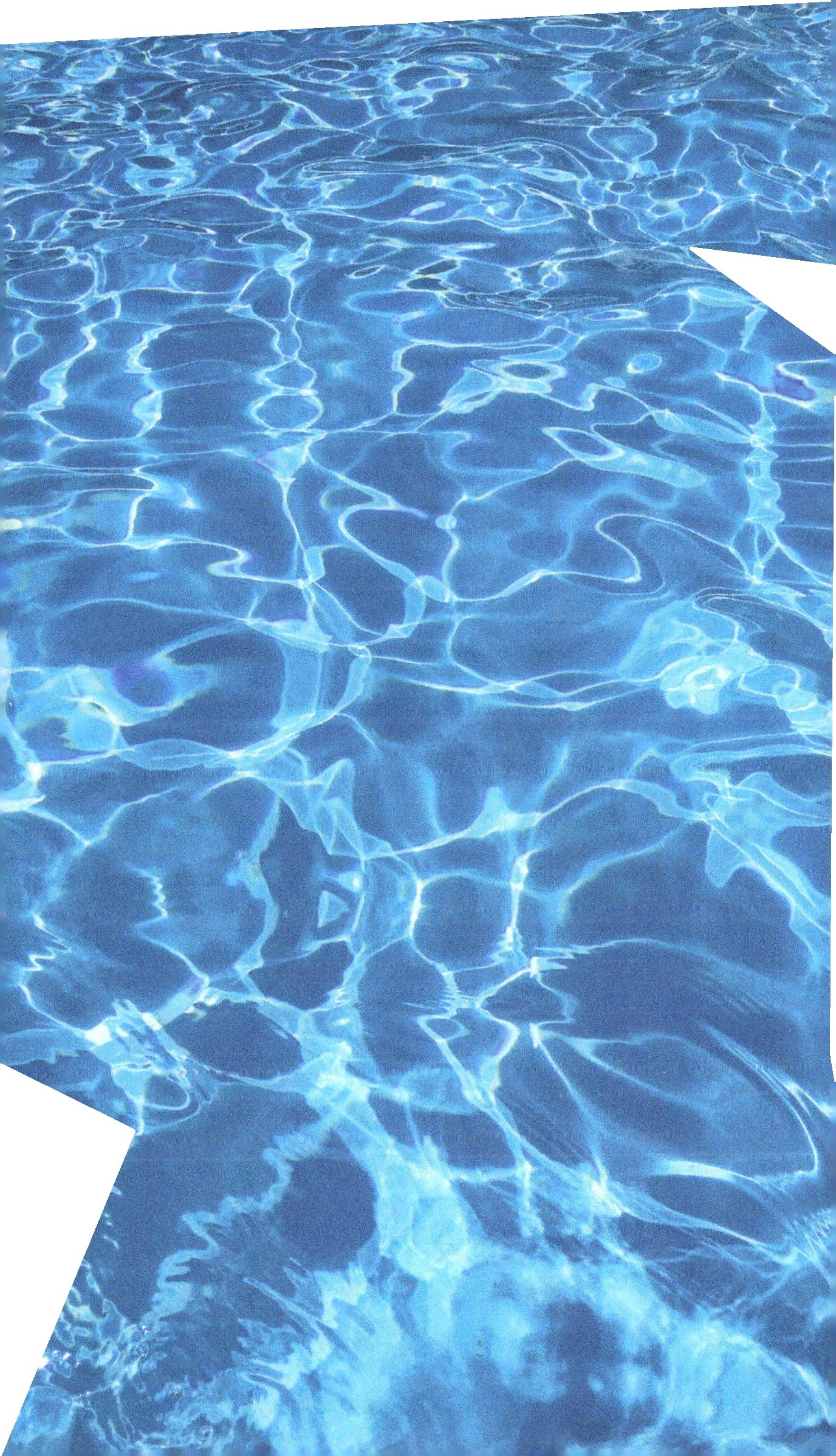

PILLAR TWO

RELAXATION / CHILL OUT

"For fast-acting relief, try slowing down."
~Lily Tomlin

RELAXATION (Noun)
The state of being free from tension and anxiety.
Synonyms: mental repose, composure,
enjoyment, leisure, amusement, fun

CHILL OUT (Adj)
Intended to induce or enhance a relaxed mood.
Synonyms: relax, loosen up, settle down, cool off

You may not realise how important relaxation is for your wellbeing. You have such a busy schedule all week, and then the weekend comes, and you don't want to waste a minute of it. You think taking time out is a luxury you don't have time for. But that's not the case. You do have time to take time out. Relaxing and chilling out makes everything better.

Me Time

Having a successful night out starts with *me* time. When you're at home getting ready, looking forward to the night ahead, and work is forgotten, for an hour or so, stay focused on you. Allow enough time so you don't rush.

Start with running a bath with candles, something you don't have time for during the work-week. Or maybe take a longer shower where you preen and spend a few more moments relaxing under the hot shower spray. It's important to have this time.

As you're in front of the mirror looking at your reflection and working out what makeup to wear with your outfit, put on your favorite music, pour a glass of wine, and just chill.

Listening to music as you're getting ready is the perfect way to relax, Choose sexy or empowering tunes. The important thing is to set up your attitude for the night ahead. Pay attention to the music you listen to while getting ready and how it makes you feel.

Also, take the time to look back and reflect on your week. Recognise that even if something went wrong, it's over. Let the emotions of a bad week fade away in this relaxing moment, as you replace them with feelings of excitement for the night ahead, in a perfect state of mind to create your dreams and desires.

If you chill out every time you get ready, it will become a ritual. Realise the power in this time to focus on you, what you really want, and the small steps you can take the following week to achieve it.

Go Off the Grid

Downtime is as important as working on your tasks and projects. It's what gives you balance and centers you. Life doesn't have to be hard. You need to take time out, connect with nature, and do things for you as often as you can, no excuses. You're more creative and better at manifesting your dreams when you're in a relaxed state.

Stress is the human body's natural response to any change in the environment that requires an

PILLAR TWO: RELAXATION / CHILL OUT

action, reaction, or adjustment to what is normal. How you handle this very much defines your stress levels.

You've no doubt experienced stress in your life due to problems with family, work, money or a bad relationship, and know the dangers of it: sickness, breakdowns, depression and serious long-term illnesses. And the more worked up you get, the harder your life becomes. Then when more bad situations seem to happen, you just can't comprehend what you've done in life to deserve this. Sound familiar?

The sayings, "Chill out" or "Hey, relax" are usually thrown around at a time when you're most stressed, and it's the last thing you need to hear from someone who doesn't have an understanding of what you're going through. Your initial response may be something a party girl on purpose should keep to herself!

It's important to understand that going off the grid every once in a while can help prevent you from getting to the point where you're stressed to the eyeballs, and I'm hoping while reading this book you're taking time out to feel more relaxed and chilled out.

So… now, while you're in this relaxed state, I'm going to say this: "YOU NEED TO CHILL OUT!"!

Say NO to Distractions

If you think you have so much to do that you can't take the time to relax, or you'll never get anything done, you'd be surprised.

You may not realise it, but you run around all day, dictated by other people's agendas. You wake up and are distracted by comments on social media and feel the need to respond. You open your email to find your inbox full of other people's to-do lists that feel as though they're designed to sabotage whatever plans you've made.

You work hard all week, and when the weekend comes around, all you want to do is let loose. This is your time to socialise and have fun. But it's only two days of the week, and you tend to overdo it. Maybe you drink too much and stay up all night, so by Monday you aren't refreshed, and you start the week feeling drained and already wishing it was Friday. You don't get productive until around Wednesday, and then it's downhill all the way to the weekend, when it starts all over again. Or you get stuck doing mundane chores all weekend and feel obliged to catch up with friends / family and never have time for yourself before Monday comes around.

PILLAR TWO: RELAXATION / CHILL OUT

This is a vicious cycle in which you don't want to be stuck in. But you can choose to break it by making sure you take time out for yourself. Yes, you have to get your work done, but in order to do this you need to say NO to distractions, NO to people demanding your time when you're getting some much-needed rest, and NO to working ridiculous amounts of overtime.

Life isn't meant to be hard. It should be engaging, fun, and playful with challenges thrown in. But you've been brought up with the belief that if you don't work hard, you won't get anywhere, and the harder you work, the more you succeed. But you must have had days when you've worked so hard, you thought you would collapse. Did you get the success results you were looking for?

Sometimes people just run from one task to another, not realising they're not getting anything done because all they're doing is putting out one fire after another. So if you wind up exhausted by the end of the day, and you realise you can't scratch off anything on your to-do list, what does that say about your productivity? Look back and figure out what distracted you from completing any of your tasks. Did you take some time for yourself to recuperate and get your bearings?

It's time to break this belief pattern and take time for yourself! You may think that by stopping and chilling out that you're wasting time, but in reality this relaxed state helps you get in the right vibration to manifest what you desire in life and recharge your energy levels, so you can tackle tasks with your full concentration.

Party girls on purpose are relaxed and fabulous. They work hard but also know when to remove their manicured foot from the gas and take some time to add balance to their life.

It's time to stop running around like a headless chicken, working hard but not getting results and living for the weekend with the intent of letting off some steam, but instead going so hard, you wind up feeling even worse Monday morning when the cycle begins again.

Every day could be an inspired day when you're on purpose. You control your time and what you do with it. When you're doing what you love, you don't need motivation to get up. You don't feel the need to escape anything and let loose every weekend, where you overdo it. Because when you're doing what you love that becomes a priority, you are excited to get things done and a hangover or fatigue getting in the way is no longer desirable. Even if you're not at your dream job right now, you pop the champagne to celebrate an achievement, not to escape a boring week. You continue working toward doing what you love and remember to take some time out to relax, so when you do go out, you can have a good time rather than using it as an escape from your unfulfilling life.

Tame the Beast

When you slow down and listen to your body and mind, you stop just using your animal instincts that may cause you to react to situations in a negative way, like flipping out if someone cuts you off, quitting your job if results don't go your way, or yelling abuse at a co-worker who says something you don't like. Once it's out there, you can't take it back.

Your animal hindbrain instincts got the better of you and made you lash out, have a knee-jerk reaction and maybe do something you deeply regret.

By chilling out, being present, and taking a few deep breaths, you recharge yourself and are able to see a situation from all sides, before you just react to it. Giving yourself time to think things through before you react and that time is valuable for preventing angry emails, rude responses and unkind words ever getting out there to do harm.

Relax and Recharge

As a party girl on purpose, you need to learn about the magic of relaxing and recharging.

PILLAR TWO: RELAXATION / CHILL OUT

Stressing never made a situation better. It spirals you downhill. But when you relax, work out your solution, and then take action, you're on the road to getting the outcome you desire in any area of your life.

People have praised the power of relaxation for centuries. Monks meditate and spend time in quiet/silent contemplation. Modern-day massage therapists and yoga instructors help you release tension and stretch your muscles. There's specific music designed to relax you and help you sleep.

Taking time to recharge is powerful. When you're in a relaxed state, you're in a higher vibration that brings you what you require to get to your destination. You may think it sounds far-fetched, but think about a time when you were stressed out while trying to complete a task or get somewhere. It either took twice as long, people or circumstances came along to get in your way, your phone died, your car was low on petrol or broke down, you missed the bus/train you needed to catch? And then you wound up saying, "WHY DOES THIS ALWAYS HAPPEN TO ME?". It's because when you're stressed, you're in a low vibration and you attract more low-vibration circumstances that will definitely block you from anything you're trying to achieve,

Now think back to when you were relaxed and attempting to complete a goal and got just the right email or phone call from someone who could help you. Or, you were in the right place at the right time to be introduced to someone who was able to supply you with the missing piece you needed. You might have thought to yourself, *I'm so lucky this happened!* But it wasn't luck. It was vibration and synchronicity. Being in the right vibration is everything. Taking time to chill out and relax puts you in the right vibration to get inspired and in alignment with what you truly want.

Chill

Get into a state where if something or someone comes along to stress you out, you don't react with a stressed response but instead take it all in and work out if it really is something to worry about, because nine times out of ten it's not going to be. Take the necessary action to get around it or avoid it, so you can get over it.

Throughout your life, you've learned what relaxes you and what stresses you out, so when you go to chill out, choose one of your learnt and trusted methods. Here's a list of some chill-outs you can try.

PILLAR TWO: RELAXATION / CHILL OUT

Examples:
Mini chill (ten-fifteen minutes)
- ★ Ten-minute meditation or guided visualisation
- ★ Ten-minute walk in nature
- ★ Ten-minute power nap
- ★ Ten-minute dip in the sea
- ★ Fifteen-minute neck and shoulder massage

Medium chill (twenty-thirty minutes)
- ★ Twenty-minute meditation or guided visualisation
- ★ Twenty-thirty minute walk or cycle in the park or a cycle
- ★ Thirty-minute back massage or facial
- ★ Thirty minutes of reading or listening to something inspirational

Maximum chill-out (forty-five minutes or longer)
- ★ Full body massage
- ★ Afternoon nap/ siesta
- ★ Yoga class

Massive chill (hour-plus)
- ★ Cycle around the park
- ★ Long walk in nature

- ★ Day at the beach, laying in the sun and swimming in the ocean
- ★ Full day spa

List your favourite ways to relax on the following pages. Then, whenever you get a spare moment, you can select one for the timeframe you've allotted and just chill out in the best way you know how. Easy!

PILLAR TWO: RELAXATION / CHILL OUT

MINI CHILLS

MEDIUM CHILLS

PILLAR TWO: RELAXATION / CHILL OUT

MAXIMUM CHILLS

MEGA CHILLS

PILLAR TWO: RELAXATION / CHILL OUT

Day after the Night before

The day after, if you've partied is more than likely going to be a low-energy day and the perfect time to chill out. Make it a duvet day and watch some inspirational movies on Netflix. David Attenborough's Nature series are perfect for this. He has a calm and soothing voice, and nature is just amazing.

If you're feeling it, head out for a walk at a beautiful location. Get some fresh air and good food. If it's the summertime, hit the beach and let that fresh, salty ocean water refresh your body and soul. Take a walk in the woods or local park.

This is the time to recover and relax, especially If you don't have anything going on. Make sure you take the time to relax. Read a book, get a massage, sleep in or Skype with friends who are far away. Allow yourself to just do nothing and don't feel guilty. These low-energy activities are good for raising your vibration, so you're in a good place to get back to work.

Summary

What if...

- ★ You set your alarm to wake you up fifteen minutes earlier than usual, did a guided meditation, and then immediately afterwards took a long shower, while spending time thinking about the day ahead and how everything will work out perfectly?
- ★ *Tip: Have your headphones already plugged into your phone by your bed, so all you have to do is press play and close your eyes. Let it sink into your subconscious. You don't have take in every word. Just let it wash over you and know something good is being taken in subconsciously, even if you nod back off.*
- ★ Instead of showering and going home after your workout, you stayed an extra fifteen minutes and used the steam room or spa to relax and wipe away the worries of the day?

PILLAR TWO: RELAXATION / CHILL OUT

* You used your lunch break to go for a walk before eating or found somewhere quiet to sit in the sun and think about how grateful you are for everything you have and how to accomplish your goals?
* You go to bed earlier and read a book that has a positive message or helps continue your personal development?

No more excuses! You now know why and how to work chill-outs into your day. Make it your goal to have it become a daily habit.

> ❝Almost anything will work again if you unplug it for a few minutes, including you.❞
> ~Anne Lamont

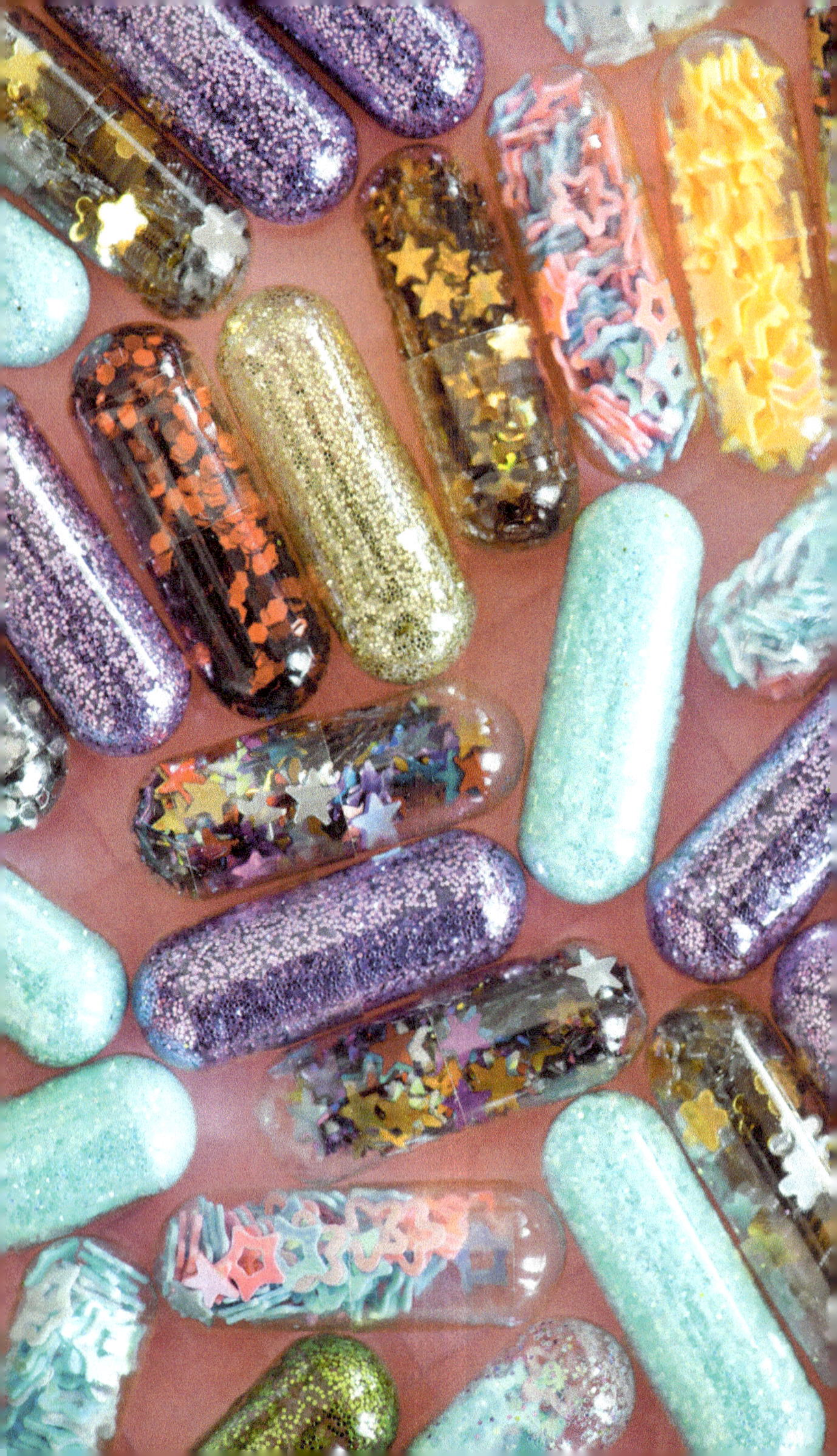

PILLAR THREE
EVALUATION / SET GOALS / INTENTIONS

❝I can never be safe. I always try and go against the grain. As soon as I accomplish one thing, I just set a higher goal. That's how I've gotten to where I am.❞
~Beyonce Knowles

EVALUATION
The making of a judgment about the amount, number, or value of something; assessment.
Synonyms: appraisal, gauging, rating, estimation, ranking, consideration, analysis, opinion

GOAL (Noun)
The object of a person's ambition or effort; an aim or desired result.

Synonyms: aim, objective, target, desired result, intention, plan, purpose

In this chapter, you get to write down what you love and truly want in life. I'm not talking about dreaming, where you just hope you'll get what you want without taking any action. This is about setting life goals and having clarity on them in order to get the universe's attention, so it knows you're serious and you know what you want.

Goals and Intentions

As a party girl, you always have goals and intentions. You have to ensure you get into the hottest club, acquire tickets to great events, and even get VIP seating. Without realising it, you're goal setting. And I'll bet nine times out of ten you got what you wanted because you had clear goals and confidence. Though you don't give yourself enough credit, you're a goal-setting master. Now, a night out might seem small scale, but imagine if you had this confidence to set life goals in all areas and go for them!

PILLAR THREE: EVALUATION / SET GOALS / INTENTIONS

Party Girl Masterminds

Goal setting can be done on your own, but a group of party masterminds coming together can create an even better energy.

While you're having pre-drinks at a friend's house, it's a good time for everyone to plan. Discuss how to make the most of your evening. How can you hit the bars and clubs at the perfect time to meet the guys and your other friends, while also catching your favorite DJ's set?

Using the strengths of each friend to create the best night out, your party girl masterminds could have the following members:

★ **The makeup artist**
That friend who can help everyone with their makeup and is the best at applying false eyelashes.
★ **The hairdresser**
The one who can help when you're having a bad hair day.
★ **The Promoter**
The one who has the contacts to get you on the guest list or jump the queues.
★ **The Hospo (hospitality)**
The one who can get free or cheap drinks

- ★ **The Wing Woman**
  The one who helps get the guy you've had your eye on
- ★ **The Big Sis**
  The one who makes sure everyone gets home safe, and if you've had too much, sends you home early.

Everyone has their strengths and value to add to the group in order to create the best nights.

Now, in terms of life goals, think about your group of friends and the skills they bring to the table. They could be great with money, have a loving relationship or are successful in their career. Rather than just using their strengths for a night out, maybe they can help in other areas of your life as well.

Just change the perspective to life goals and transfer the skills over on a bigger scale. You'll start to see how you've already been doing it. You just needed to think bigger than your night out. It's time to step up party girl!

Write Down Your Goals

We live on a planet of diversity, balance and variety. People talk about the "good old days" and forget

PILLAR THREE: EVALUATION / SET GOALS / INTENTIONS

they're living in the here and now. The best time to do or start anything is today, so what do you want to do? Here's a question that's asked at most job interviews: When you look into the future, where do you see yourself in five, ten, and thirty years from now? What legacy do you want to leave?

Have you ever really sat and down and thought that far ahead or even written down your goals? If you haven't, why not? It's fun. Daydreaming is a good start, but unless you have a goal with a plan to put it into action, that's all it will remain: a daydream. Writing down your goals and making a plan to achieve them has a lot more power and gives you something to look at and reference, in order to remind yourself of your goals and intentions. Goals are powerful. They give you something to aim for and strive towards. They clarify in your mind what you truly want and then help set the first step as to how to achieve it.

You may have no clue what your purpose is or what you really want to do with your life. Don't panic. You don't need all the answers now, but for clues you can look at your values, what you love to do, and where you spend most of your time and money. This will give you a good idea of your priorities. It took me a long time to work it out, because I never took the time to write down what I loved doing and how I enjoyed spending my time, so I could turn it into a career.

Personal development mentors teach goal setting and list writing as a very powerful practice, You set a goal and then write down a list of at least 100 reasons why achieving that goal will improve your life. You may keep a running document and keep adding to it whenever you've got a few minutes. This creates new neural pathways in the brain to help you achieve these goals once you have clearly listed and thought out how it will benefit you.

In planning the best action to take each day to achieve your goals, look at your list and pick the one goal that sparks the most feeling. Then work out the best actions steps to achieve it, and off you go. But if you don't have that list, you may not know where to start so won't get any results.

The best thing about list writing and goal setting is how easy it is. All you really need are a pen and paper.

Write down your top ten goals of what you would like right now. It could be something massive like a five-bedroom mansion in the Hollywood Hills or something as simple as a new party dress..

Mark Allen, author of *Visionary Business*, advises you to ask yourself, *If I were given $20,000,000, what*

PILLAR THREE: EVALUATION / SET GOALS / INTENTIONS

would I be doing with my life? Then he says if it isn't what you're doing right now, it's time to write down some goals and take action towards that life.

Don't fall into the trap of spending your time earning money to pay for the things you want, or think you want, while putting your dreams on hold. You let life get in the way, and before you know it, you're retiring, and you realise your dreams were never fulfilled.

This is the time to look at what you enjoy doing and what you love to spend your money on, and get it all down. Don't worry if you dream of becoming an actress, and right now the closest you've come is selling popcorn at your local cinema.

Even if you can't imagine attaining it now, you need to write it all down, so you have a clear picture in order to achieve your goals.

Remember, this is your list. If you want to see immediate results that will give you courage for bigger goals, start small. Then once you accomplish those, add another ten, until you build up to something much bigger. And if your goal is to get twenty million dollars, remember to go further and ask yourself what you would do with it. Again, too many people get money and wind up losing it, because they don't have a plan of what to do once they get it.

Have goals in all areas of your life, including relationships, finance, health and fitness, career, social and spiritual. This is such a good energy practice; it will make you feel great. It also has a mystical power. If you've heard about *The Secret*, you know they talk about Vision Boards.

John Asaraf tells the story of how he had a picture of an amazing house he wanted before he made a big name for himself. He was at the beginning of his journey in manifestation and the law of attraction, and was aiming big. Years later he was going through an old box with his son and found his board. On it was a picture of a house that wasn't just identical, it was the exact one in which he was living in. Amazing, right?!

After learning about the power of goal setting, I realised I'd unconsciously done much the same thing John Asaraf did.

When I first came to Australia with just over $1,000 to my name, I was thirty-one and sharing a room with my friend Charlie. I had nothing of value (or so I thought at the time). I wrote myself a list of what I wanted. On it was things like having my own bed, a TV, and other small items I thought would make my life better. About two years later, after discovering the law of attraction, I found the notebook I'd written in and went through,

PILLAR THREE: EVALUATION / SET GOALS / INTENTIONS

crossing off what I'd achieved without thinking about it or trying. One of them was to visit Dreamworld on the Gold Coast in Queensland, Australia. At the time I'd written it, I didn't have money to pay my rent each week, let alone afford a flight to the Gold Coast and a theme park ticket. But I achieved it when I got paid to go on tour with Silent Disco King at the Big Day Out Festival. This is when I truly discovered the power of goal setting, which spurred me on to set bigger and better goals. Masterminding with others can supply you with fresh ideas and perspectives. Work with people who possess strengths you may not have, and it will help you achieve your goals quicker.

Goal setting is fun! All you're doing is coming up with and writing down exactly what you want to attain in different areas of your life. I've had many lists throughout the years, and it's fun to go back and look over the goals I've achieved. Some happened without even realising, while others took conscious effort to attain. But since most of them have been achieved, I need to continue to upgrade and go for bigger ones.

What do you truly desire? Take some time and listen to your inner self, and maybe even meditate on the visions that are brought to mind. Then classify them into one of three categories:

- ★ Short-Term Goals
  What you want to achieve within the next six to twelve months
- ★ Medium-Term Goals
  What you want to achieve within the next five years
- ★ Long-Term Goals
  What you want to achieve within the next ten years

Once your list is complete, decide which goals will guarantee you leave a legacy. Explain why. Keep your achievements and life goals separate from your material goals. If you truly want something, list it. Don't worry if you can't imagine yourself achieving it right now. This is a work in progress. Also remember that goals can change as you evolve, and you can update your list as bigger and better goals come to mind. But at this point, just make sure you set some goals and some time lines.

If long term goals are still too big for you work on short term to medium goals to get you started and build from there, don't be put off and allow doubt to creep in work out what you truly want and get it written down somewhere for you to reference often.

It's been said that those who plan out and visualise their goals in the long-term rather than day-to-day, have a much

PILLAR THREE: EVALUATION / SET GOALS / INTENTIONS

greater chance of achievement and being a great success in life. Take time with this, and be honest with yourself.

Here are some questions to think about:

- ★ How does your life look at each of these milestones?
- ★ Who's sharing your successes with you? They may be people already in your life or ones you plan to meet. It could be your current or future partner, family, friends or business partner.
- ★ Once you achieve these goals, how do you see yourself spending your time? How are you enjoying your abundance?
- ★ Are you doing what you love to do and being paid well for it?
- ★ Are these goals helping you achieve more of what you want in life?
- ★ What skills and experiences do you want to have in your lifetime?

If you can't work some of this out yet, don't worry about it. For now just write it down and put it out there. You don't need to know how. Leave that to the universe. Being clear on your end-goal is the first step.

Material World

While many people look down on those who like to acquire material goods, if you want them, go for it. Why shouldn't you surround yourself with items that make you happy? It doesn't have to be the same for everyone. Don't be influenced by what you see in magazines as the latest "must have". Make sure your list only includes what you truly desire.

Be honest. You don't have to share your list with anyone, so be as materialistic as you like, and continue to build it as you reach your goals.

Here's an example for your material goal list:

- ★ Small Material goals:
    - ❖ Latest gadget or phone
    - ❖ New party dress
    - ❖ Lash extensions
- ★ Medium Material goals:
    - ❖ Computer
    - ❖ Three-day short course
    - ❖ Holiday to a luxury destination]
    - ❖ Louis Vuitton bag
- ★ Large Material goals:
    - ❖ House with pool and garden
    - ❖ A corner office overlooking the water

PILLAR THREE: EVALUATION / SET GOALS / INTENTIONS

- ❖ Homes all over the world
- ❖ Membership to a private jet club
- ❖ A wedding on Necker Island

Goals in All Areas

You can add goals in any category you like, such as travel, health, and finances. Get as specific as you can.

Suggestions for achievements and life goals:

- ☑ Career
- ☑ Relationships
- ☑ Finances
- ☑ Spiritual/self-improvement
- ☑ Health and wellbeing
- ☑ Skills and education

Suggestions for your material List

- ☑ Travel/Vacation
- ☑ Luxury Items
- ☑ Clothing
- ☑ Electronics
- ☑ Experiences and bucket lists

Action Steps

- [x] **Make a vision board for each list..**
  Go through magazines, cut out pictures of your goals, and pin them to your own board at home somewhere you can see it every day to remind you of your goal.

  Or with the internet, it's easy to find the pictures you're looking for, from holiday destinations to a mansion with a pool. You can print them out or keep them as your screensaver/wallpaper.

- [x] **Also get yourself a whiteboard**
  Writing your goals and achievement dates on a whiteboard is a great visual way of stating what you want and can help keep you on track with attaining them.

PILLAR THREE: EVALUATION / SET GOALS / INTENTIONS

Dreaming of goals instead of writing them down will leave you swinging at life and never achieving anything because you don't know what your aiming for.

MATERIAL GOALS

SHORT TERM

_____
_____
_____
_____
_____
_____
_____

LONG TERM

_____
_____
_____
_____
_____
_____
_____
_____

PILLAR THREE: EVALUATION / SET GOALS / INTENTIONS

CAREER GOALS

SHORT TERM

_____
_____
_____
_____
_____
_____
_____

LONG TERM

_____
_____
_____
_____
_____
_____
_____
_____

RELATIONSHIP GOALS

SHORT TERM

_____
_____
_____
_____
_____
_____
_____

LONG TERM

_____
_____
_____
_____
_____
_____
_____
_____

PILLAR THREE: EVALUATION / SET GOALS / INTENTIONS

FINANCIAL GOALS

SHORT TERM

_____
_____
_____
_____
_____
_____
_____

LONG TERM

_____
_____
_____
_____
_____
_____
_____
_____

SPIRITUAL/SELF-IMPROVEMENT GOALS

SHORT TERM

_____
_____
_____
_____
_____
_____
_____
_____

LONG TERM

_____
_____
_____
_____
_____
_____
_____
_____
_____

HEALTH AND WELLBEING GOALS

SHORT TERM

_____
_____
_____
_____
_____
_____
_____

LONG TERM

_____
_____
_____
_____
_____
_____
_____
_____

Summary

You may be wondering...

- What if I have trouble visualising my goal?
- It's okay to start small at first. Maybe downsize that trip around the world to a relaxing weekend getaway to start with.
- What if I set a goal and don't attain it by the date I specified?
- I suggest not to write them off and be honest with yourself as to how much you've been working to attain it. Maybe you have to step up the pace. Or it could be that the timeline you set was unrealistic, and you have to make it a medium or long-term goal.

> *We do not need magic to change the world, we carry all the power we need inside ourselves already: we have the power to imagine better.*
> ~J.K Rowling

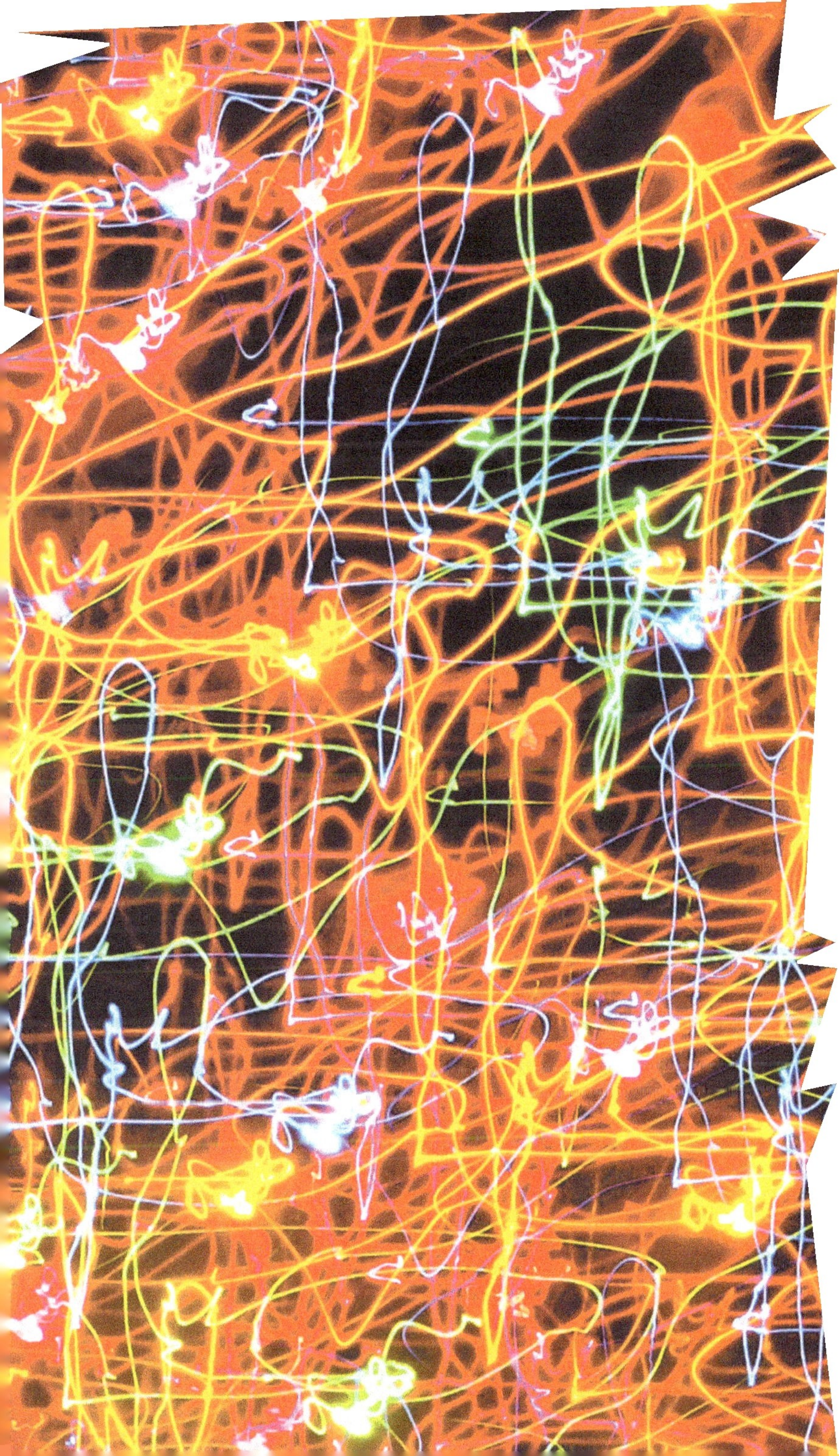

PILLAR FOUR

ACTION

❝And the day came when the risk to remain tight in a bud was more painful than the risk it took to blossom.❞
~Anaïs Nin, Author

ACTION (Noun)
The fact or process of doing something,
typically to achieve an aim.
Synonyms: measures, activity, movement,
work, effort, exertion, operation

If you weren't an action taker in the first place, you wouldn't even get off your front doorstep, let alone to any social gathering. What I mean is that you already have this skill, but now that you're starting to set quality life goals and targets, you can now take quality actions in life and not just use them to ensure a great night out.

PILLAR FOUR: ACTION

Life Rewards Action

Life rewards action. When you go on a night out, you take action without hesitation, such as deciding where to meet up, when to change venues, starting conversations with strangers, flirting with the guy you've had your eye on, and talking your way backstage or into the VIP area. It also includes your method of getting home, including if you make a detour to grab some late-night food fixes. There are lots of little actions that are part of your night out that when put together, make a great time.

You have to take action towards your goals and dreams. Some days will require hard work and long hours, but when you're striving towards your dreams, it's not the same type of hard work as it is working for someone else to help them achieve. I'm sure you understand the difference.

Lots of small actions can lead to achieving a big goal, and the key is to begin with the first step, no matter how small. Just get going. Once you start, the momentum will build, and you will begin to see results. Any frustrations or feelings of helplessness can all be overcome by taking that first small action step to creating the outcome you desire.

I can't impress this idea upon you more: *LIFE REWARDS ACTION.*

Action Equals Energy

So what is action, and how can it help you attain your goals?

Action is just energy in motion. So you could start by just getting up in the morning and going for a walk to improve your health, turning on your computer and writing the first sentence of your book, or researching a subject you're interested in pursuing. It could even be picking up the phone and calling a loved one you haven't spoken to in a while if you're lonely and feel the need to reconnect.

These actions lead to bigger ones, like completing your first whole chapter, running a marathon, or teaching, and becoming a speaker on your favourite subject. Momentum builds once action starts. Small actions lead the way to bigger ones.

It's simple, really. If you're not always learning more, developing yourself, and making constant progress, you can't be disappointed with your results. You've hit a plateau so won't get far without taking action.

Lots of little actions combined create a great night out. What little actions can you take every day to get you to your goals? Here's an action guide with an example to get you started.

PILLAR FOUR: ACTION

- ★ Goal: Take a course that will help you start your own business or a new career.
  - ❖ Action Step One: Look up courses
    Look up free courses in your area in your field of interest. Figure out what level you are at before choosing your course. If you already know the basics, you may want to take an intermediate course. Or if it's too difficult, you may want to go a step down. By researching the lesson plan, you can figure out before signing up if it's too easy or difficult for your skill level.
  - ❖ Action Step 2: Enrol
    Go for it! You'll feel so much better knowing that you've taken a major step towards your goal.
  - ❖ Action Step 3: Attend
    It seems simple, but you'd be amazed by how many people fail at this stage. If you get this far, you're already a great achiever.
  - ❖ Action Step 4: Remain present
    Learn as much as you can from the course. Take notes and participate.
  - ❖ Action Step 5: Always evolve
    Practice and apply what you've learned, and continue to grow.

Learning for Life

Too many people believe that once you leave school, you don't have to keep learning. But the world is changing and progressing at a rapid rate, and it's the people who invest in learning who will be the most successful. There's always something new to learn.

Action is procrastination's nemesis. Don't get stuck just because the next step isn't clear or seems too hard. I'm going to stress this again: life rewards action. So if something seems too hard or complicated, break it down into something more manageable that will get your desired result. Do your research. Find a mentor, who do you admire and is living a life that you would love, find out how they got there, follow them on social media and read their blogs. Be inspired by those who are achieving things in life that you would love to achieve, whether its in fitness, love, career or fame.

Start taking action, and the way will become clear. You can't steer a parked car. Sometimes you need to move first and clarity comes on the journey. You'll meet the right person or be in the right place at the right time for a golden opportunity. It's the magic of the universe. Love and appreciate every time these

PILLAR FOUR: ACTION

synchronicities happen. Action always leads to a result. Taking no action will leave you standing still, watching life pass you by.

Transfer Your Skills

Once you take small actions, you'll be inspired to take bigger ones, which will then lead to taking more and more actions. If you have a goal but feel it's too big or too out of reach, don't fret about getting immediate results. Just take one small step. Ask yourself what you can look up, who you can speak to, what small item you can buy, or what you need to learn. Then set the wheels in motion and take action towards your dreams.

You already use these skills as a party girl. Transferring them to your life goals isn't difficult when you're intentional. These are some areas where you can take your party girl skills and utilise them in other areas where you may not be satisfied:

★ Career
  Are you happy in your career? Are you getting the results you want? If not, what action steps

are you willing to take to change your career or improve the situation in your current one?

Suggested actions to improve your career, find a new one, or start a new business:

- ☑ Update your resume, so it's geared toward your dream job.
- ☑ Look up the steps to starting your own business and consult successful business owners, particularly in the area you're interested in.
- ☑ Go on interviews or auditions.
- ☑ Write a chapter of your book.
- ☑ Look into acquiring a space for your office, shop or event or set up website.
- ☑ Sign up for courses, whether in person or online, that will provide you with the needed skills to get that dream job or help you start your own business.
- ☑ Look at your hobbies and what you enjoy doing in your spare time, and figure out if you can monetise them.
- ☑ Ask for training or a promotion in your current job that could lead to a pay rise or better position.

While thinking of your current party girl skills, make a list of the skills that can transfer over to creating a business or launching a career change.

PILLAR FOUR: ACTION

★ Relationships

Are you dissatisfied with your current relationship or looking for a loving partner? What actions are you willing to take to be in a loving and satisfying relationship?

Suggested actions to find a mate or improve your current relationship:

- ☑ Sign up for a dating app and go on a couple of dates a week.
- ☑ If you're in a loving relationship, but feel like you're in a slump, rekindle the excitement of your honeymoon phase by making sure you have a date night each week or book a romantic and fun trip.
- ☑ Feel good, get a hair cut, new outfit or make-up lesson before a date.
- ☑ Go to a singles event with your friends for laughs and love prospects.

★ Finances

Do you stay on budget, or are you constantly living week to week or pay-check to pay-check? What actions are you willing to take to achieve financial independence and abundance?

These are some suggested action steps to figuring out how you can take your skills and turn them into money-makers:

- ☑ Open a savings account or get a savings app (I use Raiz) and start a small savings plan.
- ☑ If you have willpower, consider putting your money into a tin can that has to be opened with a can opener and not opening it until it's full.
- ☑ If you're spending lots of money on expensive makeup or clothes, you may want to put it away and save it for a seminar or course, to also invest in your inner world.
- ☑ On a night out, what are some of the ways you've learned to stretch a dollar while making sure everyone's needs are met?
- ☑ Are you spending money frivolously? Maybe buying drinks for everyone, so you wind up struggling the rest of the week? Your real friends will understand when you tell them you're saving for your future.

★ Health

Are you always getting ill or run down, or do you make sure you regularly get a good night's sleep, exercise and eat healthy foods? What

PILLAR FOUR: ACTION

actions would you be willing to take to have more energy, not just on party nights, but all of the time?

Suggested actions to get and stay healthy:

- ☑ Start a fitness class you enjoy or go for a run for ten or more minutes each morning.
- ☑ Drink some green juice at least twice a week and ensure you have fruit and veggies every day.
- ☑ Aim for eight hours of sleep a night.

Are you taking care of yourself after a party night, or do you walk into work exhausted on Monday morning?

You know on party nights you aren't being health conscious, so you need to make sure you rest and recuperate. When you get up the next morning, have a plan for taking care of yourself and feeling energised, so you're at your best come Monday morning.

- ★ Remember to take little steps, until you're confident enough for bigger leaps. Keep going. Don't give up, no matter what life throws at you.

Challenge yourself, so you can grow. Only listen to those who support you, and learn to ignore those who want to derail you.

New action is important, too. You may have already heard, "You will always get what you've always got if you always do what you've always done."

Don't fall into a rut. As a party girl, you know how to keep things moving. If everyone is standing around looking bored, you have ways to liven things up. You're always moving and making things better. You don't have time to worry about if it's the right move. You just get it done!

PILLAR FOUR: ACTION

If you want it you have to go for it...

ACTION WORKSHEET

Take your party girl skills and transfer them to a life goal.

List three small steps you can take each day to achieve it.

GOAL:

MONDAY

1. _____
2. _____
3. _____

TUESDAY

1. _____
2. _____
3. _____

PILLAR FOUR: ACTION

WEDNESDAY

1. _____
2. _____
3. _____

THURSDAY

1. _____
2. _____
3. _____

FRIDAY

1. _____
2. _____
3. _____

Summary

You may be wondering, what if...

- ★ You don't get the results you were hoping for?
- ★ You've tried more than one method, but it didn't seem to work?
- ★ You haven't met the right person or been offered what you need, despite feeling like you've done all you could?

Dr John Demartini says, "There's no such thing as failure. Only feedback." If the actions you've taken haven't yet gotten you the desired effect, assess your methods again to understand why and then try another way.

A party girl on purpose never stands still. She knows how to keep the night moving forward. If you can't get into one club, you know another one. If you're receiving bad service, you know who to talk to. You're the one in control of the night and know how to adapt. You don't give up and go home.

PILLAR FOUR: ACTION

You have these skills already. It's even more important when you're trying to achieve your life goals. Keep moving and taking quality actions!

❝The secret of getting ahead is getting started.❞
~Sally Berger

PILLAR FIVE
TARGET / FOCUS / NOT GIVING UP

"Having the strength to tune out negativity and remain focused on what I want gives me the will and confidence to achieve my goals."
~Gisele Bundchen

TARGET (Noun)
An objective or result towards which efforts are directed.
Synonyms: destination, objective, duty, mark, point, ambition, end, purpose, function

FOCUS (Noun)
The centre of interest or activity.
Synonyms: centre, focal point, nucleus, heart, cornerstone, linchpin, basis, anchor, backbone

Target and focus are equally important.

Target means setting a goal and continuing to aim for it until it's successfully attained. When you go out, you have your sight set on the target and don't deviate from the plan unless you have to, such as needing to switch venues. As a party girl on purpose, you're prepared for anything.

Focus is crucial, because what you focus on, you attract. If you're focused on having a good time and your night's going smoothly, you won't get distracted or put off by small mishaps that are bound to happen.

Pay Attention to Your Self-Talk

Focus doesn't mean that if you stare at the guy you fancy all night, he'll instantly be attracted to you. That just makes you look like a stalker.

What I mean is paying attention to your self-talk and what your mind is focusing on. This is the chatter that goes on inside your mind throughout the day and continues when you're lying in bed at night.

Have you ever paid attention to what it says?

For instance, is it saying good stuff like, "Congratulations on all of your successes. You look beautiful, and you're so clever"?

PILLAR FIVE: TARGET / FOCUS / NOT GIVING UP

If you're not paying attention and controlling the quality of your thoughts, I would bet it's not a supportive voice but one that points out your flaws, what you're doing wrong, and generally telling you to worry about what could happen in the future. It might fill you with fears about what other people think of you. If you're not focused, and you're allowing it to chat away, this leads to focusing on what's going wrong.

On a night out, it may be the voice that tells you that you're not as pretty as someone else, so you feel self-conscious all night. It might tell you that the guy you like would never want to talk to you, so you never go over to strike up a conversation, even though he may be thinking the same thing about you. It says that you look stupid when you dance, so you don't even go out on the dance floor when you hear your favourite tune.

Focus on What You Want

It's time to focus on what you want, where you want to be, and how you're going to get there.

If you're focusing on what you don't have or what you don't like, with no room for what you're doing well, then there's definitely some work to be done.

Abraham Hicks, (a creation of Esther and Jerry Hicks), teaches about where to focus your attention. Take a moment to think about your focus. Right now are you thinking about:

- ★ What you love and want or what you don't want?
- ★ What you do have in your life or what you don't have?

Most people unfortunately concentrate on what they don't want. They don't mean to, it is just what we have been taught. But the good news is, you can change your focus at any time, to focus on what's great and what you DO want. Now that you're aware of how your thoughts dictate your actions, you can stop that negative internal chatter and low-energy thinking at any time by putting your full focus on what you do want.

Any time you become aware you're involved in negative self-talk, try this three-step strategy:

1. Say STOP either out loud or in your mind
2. Smile to yourself, because:
   a) You've just caught yourself and become aware of your negative self- talk and stopped it in its tracks.
   b) You can't feel bad when you smile.

PILLAR FIVE: TARGET / FOCUS / NOT GIVING UP

3. Say SUCCESS! out loud or in your mind you have prevented yourself from following a negative thought pathway, and you're on your way to mastering your mind.

By following these steps, you can stop the negative self-talk and be able to carry on with your day, consciously focusing on your successes and everything that's good in your life instead.

You may have to use this method multiple times a day when you begin, but the more you do it, the better you become at stopping your negative focus and become grateful for the good stuff. Think of your mind as a muscle. You need to train it to strengthen and grow. The more you do it, the easier it becomes.

Ignore Distractions

Life moves fast. What's in one minute is out the next. You can easily become distracted by shiny objects that take your attention away from what you were originally focusing on. What all of these distractions do is prevent you from keeping your eye on your goal, your target.

Now that you have a list of goals, set your focus on them and don't allow yourself to be distracted until you've achieved them. Focus your mind to speak positively and refuse to allow negative chatter to get in your way.

Of course, there may be times when you set a goal but then feel moved to change it to something that's more meaningful to you, and that's fine. But if you keep going from one goal to the next, without ever achieving any of them, there's a problem.

Use Setbacks as Feedback

Standing out from the crowd means stick ability. Learn a skill and promote yourself to get a following of loyal customers, just like you would promote a party. It won't happen overnight, no matter what story someone is trying to sell you. If you ask anyone who's been labelled an "overnight" successes, you'll be told a long story of highs and lows, knockbacks and rejections, failures and lessons learned, before they became the sudden success they've been portrayed to be.

If you aspire to be an actress, going to your first audition and being turned down might be hard. If you're

PILLAR FIVE: TARGET / FOCUS / NOT GIVING UP

launching your first product online or opening a new store and not getting the uptake of sales and orders you had predicted, it may knock your confidence. But if you give up, all of that valuable information you learned from the experience, your schooling and networking, would go to waste. Instead, use these setbacks as feedback. Look at where you might have gotten off-track, and figure out where you can improve. Then go back to the drawing board more informed and ready.

Setbacks make you stronger and more knowledgeable. Don't underestimate the value of learning a new skill. Setbacks may not feel good at the time, and egos can be dented or knocked. It's okay to have the belief that you're the best and deserve recognition, but don't be too self-obsessed and think you know everything.

Always be willing to grow and learn. If you don't better yourself, you can get left behind and become stagnant and set in your ways. Always aim to grow and be better. Remain focused on your goals and enjoy them once they're achieved, before moving on to the next bigger, better one.

Imagine a life with no boredom or monotony, just achievement. How exciting and amazing does that sound! Rest when you need downtime. Learn about yourself and what you're interested in, and always be willing to grow bigger and stay focused, with your eye constantly on the prize.

Become an Expert

Pere Bristow is a famous singing coach from LA who believes anyone can be trained to hold a note, even if they're tone deaf, and that talent is only a small part of the equation. The desire to achieve a dream is the key.

Once that goal is identified, give it your all to achieving it. If your dream is to be a singer, you have to get up every day and sing. Get training from other talented people, and practice, practice, practice. This is what it takes. There may be long hours, and for a time you might have to give up some activities you enjoy, but if at the end if it meant being a successful singer, I'm sure you'd agree all of that hard work was worth it!

You need to believe in yourself, and go out there do your best.

According to Dr Demartini, no matter how old you are, if you study for one hour every day for three years, you'll be an expert in that subject. Now that doesn't sound too hard, does it?

PILLAR FIVE: TARGET / FOCUS / NOT GIVING UP

There will always be challenges. Other people or factors that will try and put you off track. Some say this is the universe testing you to find out if this is really what you really want. If you continue on through the challenging times when you want to give up, you will reach new heights of achievement.

In the book *Think and Grow Rich*, there's a story about a gold prospector who spent years mining for gold but never got the big payout. He invested his time and energy and 'knew' there was a large vein of gold in the area but gave up before he found it. He sold his equipment and mine off at a bargain price, only for the next person to find the gold within a matter of weeks. If the prospector had just kept going, he would have found the treasure, but he lost his belief.

Star Power

Did you know that in 1993, Beyoncé and Kelly Rowland, both aged seven at the time, lost in the *Star Search* competition? Then they got a record deal with Elektra records that they lost in 1996 before they even had had the chance to create music. Through family issues, they continued on, and after many changes to their line-up and animosity, they found success and continued to go from strength to strength, until Destiny's Child wound up being one of the biggest girl groups, and Beyoncé is undoubtedly one of the top female artists of all time.

What if they'd thrown in the towel when the going got tough and they were dropped from their record label?

Jennifer Lopez (J-LO) started off as a dancer and went against her mother's wishes to pursue a dance career. She wound up sleeping on a couch at her dance studio and living off a slice of pizza a day. Then she became one of the Fly Girls on *In Living Color* and found fame and success as an actress and singer. And though she's had relationship issues and a failed fashion label, she never gave up, and is a household name with many successes under her belt, still going strong and a great role model for many young girls.

Katy Perry is the most followed star on Twitter and has had many number one hits and albums, but she comes from a family that only allowed her to listen to Christian music. She used to sneak her favorite popular music CDs, like Nirvana, from her friends to listen to and began vocal lessons at age nine. She then released a gospel album that sold around two-hundred copies only and she was also dropped by Def Jam records and Columbia, before she was signed by Capitol in 2007

PILLAR FIVE: TARGET / FOCUS / NOT GIVING UP

and released "I Kissed a Girl" in 2008. And the rest is history. If she'd given up after the first album, so many great songs, and an amazing entertainer, would not be in the world right now making your day brighter.

J.K. Rowling, the author of *Harry Potter*, was in the middle of a divorce in from a short-term marriage, and in her own words was as poor as you could be in modern Britain without being homeless. Struggling to pay bills and feed her daughter, she dreamed of being an author, something her parents thought was a quirk that would never pay the mortgage or give her a retirement fund.

But she said hitting rock bottom meant she knew how bad it could be, so she set to work doing what she knew was her calling and wrote *Harry Potter and the Philosopher's Stone*, which sold over four-hundred-million copies and became the fastest-selling book of all time, making J.K. Rowling a billionaire, a title which she has now lost due to charitable donations. She's an amazing example of getting clear on what you want and staying on track no matter what life throws at you.

And even though this book is dedicated to girl power, I would like to add Ed Sheeran to this list of international stars who set goals, took plenty of action and stayed on target until they reached them. I admire him so much and think he's an amazing human being.

Ed was bullied as a child for his hair colour, stutter, and large glasses. He struggled with his speech until he gave up trying to talk in public. But he loved music and would sing in his church choir and practice with his guitar in his room.

He knew his future was in music. His dad brought him Eminem's first album when he was nine, and Ed was blown away with how he could rap so fast and learnt every rap word for word before writing his own raps and songs, until he conquered his stutter.

Then he set out busking and performing in pubs, often doing twelve gigs a week, and sleeping on sofas where he could crash. When they weren't available, he slept on the street and often went without food.

He knew America was where he could make his dreams come true and set off without a recording contract. He sent his music to every radio station but heard nothing, until a DJ got him on stage at a live poetry event. The crowd wasn't sure what to make of him at first, but within the first song he had everyone swaying and clapping along. That DJ was Jamie Foxx, who was so impressed by Ed he let him sleep on his couch (if you're going to sleep on a couch, then Jamie Foxx's would be a good one to be on) and use his recording studio. From then on, he created music until

PILLAR FIVE: TARGET / FOCUS / NOT GIVING UP

he got a call from his current BFF, Taylor Swift, who asked him to tour with her. Ed as of writing this book is ranked the ninth highest-paid celebrity in the world and is one of the nicest guys in music.

There are probably many amazing stars and talents out there we will never see or hear because they didn't remain focused and stayed on target until they achieved their goal. Don't let that person be you. If you have a passion and believe in your gifts, then go for it, and keep going through the hard times.

Stay on the path to your goal, don't let challenges or anyone get in your way.

DECLARE IT

You're now going to take your top goals and make a commitment to stay on target and focused until you complete them. Give this goal a completion date and a reward if you attain it.

Small goals might have a short date target of a week or a month with a small reward, while bigger goals may take six months to a year.

Focus on what you do want, and when you feel your mind wandering to negative thoughts or outcomes, stop and get back on track to what's going well.

This may be hard at first if you've never consciously listened or paid attention to where your mind is focused, but with practice, you can change it into a positive influence. Stay focused on the good things in life. When you've mastered that, there's no holding you back.

There is also a version of the declaration form you can download at partygirlsonpurpose.com

PILLAR FIVE: TARGET / FOCUS / NOT GIVING UP

Declaration
OF COMMITMENT

I

Commit to achieving

By the date of

By dedication to

and service of

I will celebrate the achievement by

Sincerely,

www.partygirlsonpurpose.com
@partygirlsonpurpose   /partygirlsonpurpose
/partygirlsonpurpose

Summary

Ask yourself: What if...

- ★ You practiced or worked on your goal for just one hour today?
- ★ You view setbacks as feedback and come up with a better way to achieve it?
- ★ You paid attention to your internal chatter, stopped it when it became negative, and replaced the thought with a positive one?

If you get knocked down, come back harder, jump up quicker, and keep on going. You're a party girl on purpose, and you can do anything.

> *I don't put the focus on things that don't matter.*
> **~Alessia Cara**

Party Queen and Boss Babe Final Thoughts

My wish is for you is to believe you can do, be, and achieve anything you desire. You're a fun-loving, socially aware lady who has so much to give and understands the benefits of celebrating life, and most of all, being the beautiful person you are!

If you've completed the workbook pages, congratulations! You have everything you need to get on purpose and start taking action towards the life you love. So don't let anybody or anything get in your way.

If you haven't started, it's okay. Just remember that the best time to plant an acorn is today. If you're looking for better results in your life, you need to do the work and start taking quality actions. Life rewards action, so just start with one exercise, and remember to keep adding and refining your lists to create your beautiful and fabulous life.

Set aside time to go back and fill in the action points for each chapter.

You're the life of the party and successful at it, so it's not going to be difficult to make a few small changes to the skills you've honed as a party girl and use them to achieve an amazing life.

These are the key messages I'd like you to take away:

- ★ **Be grateful**

  Be thankful for even the smallest things in your life. If you're struggling, get back to basics. Pick one simple thing to be grateful for, like being alive to experience another day on this beautiful planet, and keep expanding your list. By appreciating what you have, you're opening yourself up to receiving so much more.

- ★ **Relax**

  Take time to chill out, whether it's doing meditation, listening to music or going for a walk in nature. Anything that focuses on you, makes you feel good, and puts you in a relaxed state to manifest and create the life you really want to live.

- ★ **Evaluate**

  Get clear on where you want to go and what you want to have. Write down your goals, create a vision board/goals board, give yourself a timeline, and cover all areas in order to make sure the universe understands in clear terms what you would like it to bring to you.

- ★ **Action**

  Life rewards action, so take that first step towards your goal, and then another. Before you know it, you'll achieve the success you dream of.

- ★ **Target**

  Stay focused on your goals. People and situations will come along to get in your way, but keep on track and continue to take small actions towards your goals, and the path will become clear. There is no failure, only feedback.

- ★ **Focus**

  Concentrate on what's amazing in your life. Don't let negative self-talk rule you. Take back your thoughts. Be aware of what you're focusing your energy on, because this is where it flows. Remain attentive, and make sure you declare what you really want.

As a reader of this book, you have access to the *Party Girls on Purpose* private Facebook group, to join other fun and fantastic party girls on purpose who are helping one another take action and stay on track.

Please share your victories, what you're thankful for, and how you've used these principles to set and manifest your goals.

I'll be there to answer your questions and give you tips if you lose your way, want advice and help you celebrate your successes.

I hope you've found value in these pages and an inspiration to shift your mindset into believing you can achieve anything. Remember that life's not just to be enjoyed two days of the week. Every day should be fun. When you take time to work out what you truly love to do and how to achieve it, you're on your way to never working another day in your life.

This may be the start of your journey into self-development that will lead you to learning at a deeper level about the law of attraction, manifesting, and the magic of the universe we live in.

I hope you seek out more great teachers and find the confidence to replace negative thoughts with positive ones and turn your dreams into reality.

Have fun, love life, celebrate you're successes, and forever be a fabulous PARTY GIRL ON PURPOSE.

About the author

Partying hard at weekends, stuck in unfulfilling jobs and yet living a life that allowed her to rub shoulders with superstars Calvin Harris and Ed Sheeran, Lauren Ellingham's previous life was often glamorous – yet despite all this she felt stuck in a life that wasn't meant for her.

Fast-forward a decade and Lauren's now travelling the world, living between Uk, Australia and Bali, a successful business owner and an author. Her first book *Party Girls On Purpose*, draws on her life experience to provide an awe-inspiring yet practical guide for women wanting to unlock the potential within and live the life they crave.

It's a self-help book but not as you know it, it's more a modern-day life guide that outlines the five GREAT principles party girls use on a night out that are needed to achieve the ultimate in personal success. In detail she explains how gratitude, relaxation chilling out, evaluation, action and staying focus and on track are key to success in life.

But what motivated Lauren to write *Party Girls On Purpose*? Well, for years and across many continents Lauren worked mainly in order to party hard all weekend, usually waking up less than fresh. And despite an enviable life in the UK music event industry, she was stuck in a rut and living week-to-week.

She decided to move to Australia, and when she arrived with just $1400 in her pocket, she was determined to leave her old life behind make her way to the top.

It was a rocky start, but she sought training from personal development experts such as Dr John DeMartini from *The Secret* and Carl Harvey; who was the head copywriter at MindValley, and willingly became a student to improve her results in life.

Lauren also invested time and money in herself in order to harness what she had learned over the years to help others.

She also sought out mentors with credible teachers such as Benjamin J Harvey of Authentic Education, the only personal development company in Australia to make the BRW fast starters list.

Every step of the way Lauren's been determined to use her knowledge to help women realise they can get

ABOUT THE AUTHOR

anything they want in life. Such is her own ambition and drive, in just her second year of owning and directing Silent Disco King Australia, she was asked to tour with Australia's biggest touring music festival, Big Day Out.

She got to party among musical greats and superstars such as Snoop Dog and Robert Patterson. It was something she visualised when she first landed in Australia and to have it happen was a life-changing experience.

Set backs and challenges have still come along but a disastrous event to some, like losing her visa for Australia through unscrupulous bosses didn't phase her. Everything she had learnt had shown her the universe has her back. She wants to teach this confidence to you too.

No longer a slave to a life she didn't love, Lauren's now as passionate as ever about giving women the freedom and power to be successful in whatever they put their mind to. And she can't wait to have you along for the ride – it's going to be amazing!

To get in touch with Lauren shoot her an email to Lauren@partygirlsonpurpose.com or keep up-to-date with her current events by visiting her website www.partygirlsonpurpose.com or Facebook page

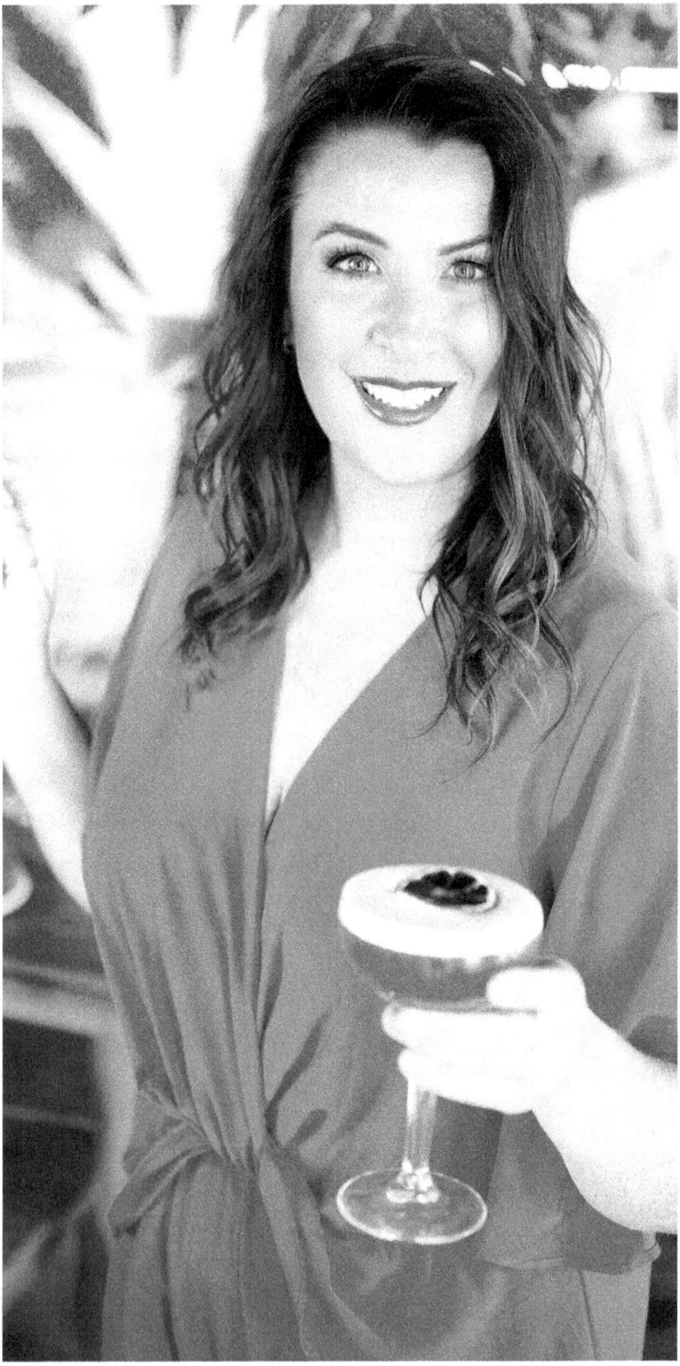

REFERENCES TO THE SOURCES OF THE QUOTES MENTIONED IN THE BOOK

Melody Beattie – Melody Beattie is one of America's most beloved self-help authors and a household name in addiction and recovery circles.

Her international bestselling book, Codependent No More, introduced the world to the term "codependency" in 1986.

Millions of readers have trusted Melody's words of wisdom and guidance because she knows firsthand what they're going through.

In her lifetime, she has survived abandonment, kidnapping, sexual abuse, drug and alcohol addiction, divorce, and the death of a child. "Beattie understands being overboard, which helps her throw bestselling lifelines to those still adrift," said Time Magazine.

Oprah Winfrey – Oprah Winfrey born Orpah Gail Winfrey January 29, 1954 is an American media executive, actress, talk show host, television producer and philanthropist. She is best known for her talk show The Oprah Winfrey Show, which was the highest-rated television program of its kind in history and was nationally syndicated from 1986 to 2011 in Chicago. Dubbed the "Queen of All Media", she was the richest African American of the 20th century and North America's first black multi-billionaire, and has been ranked the greatest black philanthropist in American history. She has also been sometimes ranked as the most influential woman in the world.

Lily Tomlin – Mary Jean "Lily" Tomlin (born September 1, 1939) is an American actress, comedian, writer, singer, and producer. Tomlin began her career as a stand-up comic as well as performing Off-Broadway during the 1960s. Her breakout role was on the variety show Rowan & Martin's Laugh-In from 1969 until 1973. She currently stars on the Netflix series Grace and Frankie as Frankie Bergstein; the role has garnered her four consecutive Emmy nominations since 2015.

Anne Lamont – Anne Lamott (born April 10, 1954) is an American novelist and non-fiction writer.

She is also a progressive political activist, public speaker, and writing teacher. Lamott is based in Marin County, California, her nonfiction

REFERENCES TO THE SOURCES OF THE QUOTES MENTIONED IN THE BOOK

works are largely autobiographical. Marked by their self-deprecating humor and openness, Lamott's writings cover such subjects as alcoholism, single-motherhood, depression, and Christianity.

Beyonce Knowles Carter – Beyoncé Giselle Knowles-Carter born September 4, 1981) is an American singer, songwriter, and actress. Born and raised in Houston,Texas, Beyoncé performed in various singing and dancing competitions as a child. She rose to fame in the late 1990s as lead singer of the R&B girl-group Destiny's Child. Managed by her father, Mathew Knowles, the group became one of the world's best-selling girl groups in history. Their hiatus saw Beyoncé's theatrical film debut in Austin Powers in Goldmember (2002) and the release of her debut album, Dangerously in Love (2003). The album established her as a solo artist worldwide, debuting at number one on the US Billboard 200 chart and earning five Grammy Awards, and featured the Billboard Hot 100 number one singles "Crazy in Love" and "Baby Boy".

J.K. Rowling – Joanne Rowling "rolling" born 31 July 1965, writing under the pen names J.K. Rowling and Robert Galbraith, is a British novelist, philanthropist, film producer, television producer and screenwriter, best known for writing the Harry Potter fantasy series. The books have won multiple awards, and sold more than 500 million copies, becoming the best-selling book series in history. They have also been the basis for a film series, over which Rowling had overall approval on the scripts and was a producer on the final films in the series.

Born in Yate, Gloucestershire, England, Rowling was working as a researcher and bilingual secretary for Amnesty International when she conceived the idea for the Harry Potter series while on a delayed train from Manchester to London in 1990. The seven-year period that followed saw the death of her mother, birth of her first child, divorce from her first husband and relative poverty until the first novel in the series, Harry Potter and the Philosopher's Stone, was published in 1997.

Rowling has lived a "rags to riches" life story, in which she progressed from living on state benefits to being the world's first billionaire author. She lost her billionaire status after giving away much of her earnings to charity, but remains one of the wealthiest people in the world. She is the United Kingdom's bestselling living author, with sales in excess of £238M

REFERENCES TO THE SOURCES OF THE QUOTES MENTIONED IN THE BOOK

Anaïs Nin – Angela Anaïs Juana Antolina Rosa Edelmira Nin y Culmell (February 21, 1903 – January 14, 1977), known professionally as Anaïs Nin was a French-American diarist, essayist, novelist, and writer of short stories and erotica. Born to Cuban parents in France, Nin was the daughter of composer Joaquín Nin and Rosa Culmell, a classically trained singer. Nin spent her early years in Spain and Cuba, about sixteen years in Paris (1924–1940), and the remaining half of her life in the United States, where she became an established author.

Amelia Mary Earhart – (born July 24, 1897; disappeared July 2, 1937) was an American aviation pioneer and author. Earhart was the first female aviator to fly solo across the Atlantic Ocean. She received the United States Distinguished Flying Cross for this accomplishment. She set many other records, wrote best-selling books about her flying experiences and was instrumental in the formation of The Ninety-Nines, an organization for female pilots. In 1935, Earhart became a visiting faculty member at Purdue University as an advisor to aeronautical engineering and a career counselor to women students. She was also a member of the National Woman's Party and an early supporter of the Equal Rights Amendment.

Gisele Bundchen – Gisele Caroline Bündchen (Portuguese:, German: born 20 July 1980) is a Brazilian model and actress.

Since 2004, Bündchen has been among the highest-paid models in the world, and as of 2007 was the 16th richest woman in the entertainment industry. In 2012, she placed first on the Forbes top-earning models list. In 2014, she was listed as the 89th Most Powerful Woman in the World by Forbes.

In the late 1990s, Bündchen was the first in a wave of Brazilian models to find international success. In 1999, Vogue noted "The Return of the Sexy Model", and she was credited with ending the "heroin chic" era of modeling. Bündchen was one of the Victoria's Secret Angels from 2000 until mid-2007. Bündchen pioneered the "horse walk", a stomping movement created when a model picks her knees up high and kicks her feet out in front. In a 2007 Vogue interview, Claudia Schiffer stated that Bündchen is the only remaining supermodel.

Alessia Cara – Alessia Caracciolo (Italian: born July 11, 1996), known professionally as Alessia Cara, is a Canadian singer and songwriter. After producing acoustic covers, she signed with EP Entertainment and Def Jam Recordings in 2014 and released her

REFERENCES TO THE SOURCES OF THE QUOTES MENTIONED IN THE BOOK

debut single the following year, "Here", which reached number 19 on the Canadian Hot 100 chart and was a sleeper hit in the United States, peaking at number 5 on the Billboard Hot 100 chart.

Cara's debut studio album, Know-It-All (2015), reached number 8 on the Canadian Albums Chart and number 9 on the Billboard 200 chart in the United States. The album's third single, "Scars to Your Beautiful", reached number 8 on the Billboard Hot 100 in 2016. In 2017, Cara collaborated with DJ and producer Zedd to create the single "Stay", and with rapper Logic to feature in his song "1-800-273-8255". Cara has received nominations for four Grammy Awards, including a win for Best New Artist in 2018.

John Fredrick Demartini – (born November 25, 1954), is an American researcher, best selling author, international educator, public speaker in human behavior and former chiropractor.

He founded the Demartini Institute and has trademarked certain methodologies in human development, the primary two being the Demartini Method and the Demartini Value Determination Process.

Demartini has also appeared in several films, including The Secret in 2006.

Esther Hicks – (née Weaver, born March 5, 1948) is an American inspirational speaker and author. She has co-written nine books with her husband Jerry Hicks, presented numerous workshops on the law of attraction with Abraham Hicks Publications and appeared in the original version of the 2006 film The Secret. The Hicks' books, including the series The Law of Attraction, are — according to Esther Hicks — "translated from a group of non-physical entities called Abraham." Hicks describes what she is doing as tapping into "infinite intelligence".

John Assaraf – has built 5 multimillion dollar companies, written 2 New York Times Bestselling books and featured in 8 movies, including the blockbuster hit "The Secret" and "Quest For Success" with Richard Branson and the Dalai Lama.

Today, he is founder and CEO of NeuroGym, a company dedicated to using the most advanced technologies and evidence based brain training methods to help individuals unleash their fullest potential and maximize their results.

Carl James Harvey – After getting his law degree Carl decided it wasn't for him and wanted the four hour work week so he could sip cocktails on the beach. He created that life then realsied he wanted more.

REFERENCES TO THE SOURCES OF THE QUOTES MENTIONED IN THE BOOK

Moving to Kuala Lumpur to work as head copy writer at Mindvalley Carl now has his own business with his, Abundance Bookclub, Inner circle Group and Abundance TV. He works with hundreds of people worldwide who want to start their own businesses to help others.

With his swaggy clothes, love for rap music and champagne Carl has a unique way of delivering his message that's all about the high vibes and abundance.

Benjamin J Harvey: Difference-Maker Mentor – Through his company Authentic Education, Benjamin has helped tens of thousands of people craft a life filled with purpose, passion, and love — regardless of where they have come from, where they are today, or where they are going.

However, it wasn't always that way. Not too long ago, Benjamin found himself:

More than $137,000 in debt
Weighing over 120kg
Depressed and directionless

Until he took one vital step and bought $17,995 worth of education that changed the trajectory of his life, compelling him to lose weight, get out of debt, clear his depression and spend the next 20 years traveling across the planet on a mission!

A mission giving him a purpose that helped him discover some of the deepest mysteries of the human mind, body, and spirit and create a life that has seen him:

His company was the Australian BRW Fast-Start award in 2013 and BRW Fast 100 award in 2015

Glossary

Affirmations – the act or an instance of affirming state of being affirmed. It is the assertion that something exists or is true. Something that is affirmed a statement or proposition that is declared to be true. Confirmation or ratification of the truth or validity of a prior judgment, decision, etc. Law. a solemn declaration accepted instead of a statement under oath.

Magic – the power of apparently influencing events by using mysterious or supernatural forces. "Suddenly, as if by magic, the doors start to open"

Law of Attraction (LOA) – is the attractive, magnetic power of the Universe that draws similar energies together. It manifests through the power of creation, everywhere and in many ways. Even the law of gravity is part of the law of attraction. This law attracts thoughts, ideas, people, situations and circumstances.

Manifestation – is a manifestation is the public display of emotion or feeling, or something theoretical made real. Manifestation's origins are in religion and spirituality because if something spiritual becomes real, it is said to be a manifestation. The word's usage has spread to include all aspects of life.

Personal Development – it covers activities that improve awareness and identity, develop talents and potential, build human capital and facilitate employability, enhance the quality of life and contribute to the realization of dreams and aspirations. Personal development takes place over the course of a person's entire life. Not limited to self-help, the concept involves formal and informal activities for developing others in roles such as teacher, guide, counselor, manager, life coach or mentor. When personal development takes place in the context of institutions, it refers to the methods, programs, tools, techniques, and assessment systems that support human development at the individual level in organizations.

The Magic – is a 2012 self-help and spirituality book written by Rhonda Byrne. It is the third book in *The Secret* series. The book was released on March 6, 2012, as a paperback and e-book. The book is available in 41 languages.

CPSIA information can be obtained
at www.ICGtesting.com
Printed in the USA
LVHW010149140520
655469LV00006B/149

9 781925 471366